FINDING ITHAKA

A Modern Odyssey Across Continents

GEORGE THEOTOCATOS

FINDING ITHAKA: A Modern Odyssey Across Continents
© 2019
By George Theotocatos

This work is a nonfiction memoir. It reflects the author's present recollection of experiences over time. While the stories in this book are true, some characteristics have been changed and dialogue reconstructed to best reflect the veracity of the events that occurred.

ISBN-13: 9781794259607

Editor: Gina Mazza
Cover Design: Lee Ann Fortunato-Heltzel
Cover Art: Diana Antonakatou (1922 - 2012), watercolor,
The Island of Ithaka
Photos: George Theotocatos' personal collection

George Theotocatos
East Hampton, New York
gtheoto@yahoo.com

ITHAKA

By C. P. Cavafy; Collected Poems (Princeton University Press, 1975)
Translated by Edmund Keeley

As you set out for Ithaka
hope the road is a long one,
full of adventure, full of discovery.
Laistrygonians, Cyclops,
angry Poseidon—don't be afraid of them:
you'll never find things like that on your way
as long as you keep your thoughts raised high,
as long as a rare excitement
stirs your spirit and your body.
Laistrygonians, Cyclops,
wild Poseidon—you won't encounter them
unless you bring them along inside your soul,
unless your soul sets them up in front of you.

Hope your road is a long one.
May there be many a summer morning when,
with what pleasure, what joy
you enter harbors you're seeing for the first time;
may you stop at Phoenician trading stations
to buy fine things,
mother of pearl and coral, amber and ebony,
sensual perfume of every kind—

as many sensual perfumes as you can;
and may you visit many Egyptian cities
to learn and go on learning from their scholars.

Keep Ithaka always in your mind.
Arriving there is what you're destined for.
But don't hurry the journey at all.
Better if it lasts for years,
so you're old by the time you reach the island,
wealthy with all you've gained on the way,
not expecting Ithaka to make you rich.

Ithaka gave you the marvelous journey.
Without her you wouldn't have set out.
She has nothing left to give you now.

And if you find her poor, Ithaka won't have fooled you.
Wise as you will have become, so full of experiences,
you'll have understood by then what these Ithakas mean.

———————————

C. P. Cavafy (1863 - 1933) was a Greek poet who was born and lived in Alexandria, Egypt to Greek parents. He is widely accepted as the most distinguished Greek poet of the 20th Century. His most famous poem, Ithaka, written in 1911, was inspired by the Homeric return of Ulysses (Odysseus) to his native Greek island.

DEDICATION

To my granddaughters:
Penelope, Zoe, Maya and Abigail

CONTENTS

PART THREE: Years in the Middle East

PART FOUR: A New Life After Retirement

PART FIVE: My Family's Voices

PART SIX: Ancestry Tree

INTRODUCTION

I have wanted to write the story of my family for some time but something always got in the way of getting started—until now. In September 2017, my daughter, Daphne, and her husband, Chris, retained historian David O'Neil to interview me and Chris' father, Ed, about our family history. The audio of my interview was completed two months later and distributed to my children and grandchildren. That process provided the spark to write this book so that I could share my life story in greater detail for posterity.

The stories in this book retrace the journeys and lives of family members spanning five generations. Some of these events happened many years ago and, as such, I have relied on my best recollections of them. Others are as fresh in my mind as if they occurred yesterday. The narrative moves from continent to continent and describes an ever-changing world as my ancestry, family and relatives left their homes of origin and settled in new unknown places. In doing so, they created opportunities for themselves and their children through hard, honest work. While it is impossible to retell all details of a life in one book, I recount real stories that capture many of the most memorable events, high and low points, and multi-various experiences that have comprised our travels through life, both literally and metaphorically.

The book cover, which portrays the island of Ithaka, provides a prologue for the narrative that follows. In choosing the book's title, I was inspired by the famous Greek poet from Alexandria. C. P. Cavafy's epic poem, Ithaka, symbolizing a person's long journey through life towards a destination . . . but at the end, like Cavafy suggests, it's not only the goal but the journey itself that matters, because the voyage makes us wiser, more experienced and knowledgeable.

To round out the narrative, I've cobbled together the best family photos I could find, along with other noteworthy clippings of ancestral memorabilia that enhance the story with imagery.

Part Five gives voice to several other family members. I've asked my brother, Takis, and cousins, John Barbas and John Deligeorges and his daughter Joanne, to share their stories and remembrances, as well. I also would be remiss if I didn't include my father's short stories and poems that my son, Nicholas, wrote over the years. So this book is a true creative collaboration of various loved ones. While writing these pages, I researched our family tree; it is included in Part Six.

These chapters may be read in chronological order, or you may prefer to skip around. I have written them in such a way that each chapter stands alone but they can be read together, as a blending of the past and present.

My ancestors and my generation maintained their Greek origin, culture and language even though at least three generations, from both sides of my family, were born and lived outside the national boundaries of Greece. My children and two of my grandchildren were born in America and the other two of my grandchildren are Americans, born in Austria and South Africa. So as it turns out, we are indeed a global family with American roots—or, perhaps, an American family with global roots.

The world of my grandparents' generation was much different than the world my children have grown up in, and I suspect that my grandchildren's lives will be equally as different. But we all share a common goal: a commitment to a higher purpose and to provide a better, safer future for our children. My wish is that what I've documented here will ignite a similar spark of interest for my beautiful granddaughters—Penelope (Penny), Zoe, Maya and Abigail (Abby)—to explore and ask questions, to seek and find answers about who their ancestors were, how they lived and why we are where we are today. It is important to know one's roots, the sacrifices of those who came before, and on whose shoulders we still proudly stand.

Beyond the humble retelling of my family's history, this is a story of the human spirit, its endurance and quest for a better life. It is a testimony to achieving personal excellence under adverse conditions through hard work, taking risks, pushing one's edge, always learning new skills and appreciating the opportunities one is given. I am a fortunate man in this regard, as my life has been fully and well lived. God has been good to my family and me, and I am thankful for His blessings.

PART ONE
A Greek From Egypt

1

An Island in the Nile

"Oh, so you are Egyptian."

This is the typical reaction I get when I meet someone for the first time and say that I was born in Egypt. That's when I have to carefully explain that I am a Greek who happened to be born in Egypt from Greek parents.

"I guess you could say I'm a Greek from Egypt," I usually respond. I prefer this description because it identifies both my national heritage and birthplace.

To be precise, I was born on Fisher Island in the middle of the River Nile, 100 miles south of Cairo. How my parents ended up there is a tale of destiny. My father, Nicholas Theotocatos, was born in Smyrna, Turkey and my mother, Stella Barbas, was born in Cairo. Both of their families immigrated to Egypt, where my parents eventually met when my father was forty years old and my mother was twenty-seven.

At the time of their marriage, my father worked for a rich Egyptian, a Pasha, by the name of Mohamed Sharawi. "Pasha" is a royal title in Egypt, a tradition inherited from the Ottoman Empire. The elite structure of the kingdom included the king at the top and the "Pashas" and "Beys" below. I will not get into how this system worked but suffice to say that the structure was firmly established with all the perks that come along with rank, and Sharawi enjoyed many of them.

In fact, Sharawi owned a tropical island that was mostly a mango plantation. He hired my father to live there and be the general manager of the plantation. Within a few months of being married, my mother became pregnant with me; I was born in 1938, a year after they wed. During the last three months of the pregnancy, Mom stayed with my grandparents in Cairo. Shortly after giving birth, she rejoined my father on the island with me in tow.

We lived in the only large structure on the island, a huge old historic house in the middle of a dense forest of mango trees. The only means for getting to the island was to take a traditional riverboat called a *felucca*. These boats are comprised of a single large sail and a flat bottom. The only inhabitants on the island were a few plantation workers. There was little communication with the outside world and no basic utilities like electricity or city water. Being a new wife and young mother, Mom was lonely most of the time, with no friends or family nearby, but she made the best of the situation.

Fisher Island

When I was older, my mother told me stories about life on the island, particularly how they lived in constant fear of floods. There were countless days of ongoing vigilance, anxiously watching the level of the Nile rise precariously during the rainy season. Normally, it took 121 steps to walk from the boat dock to land. During flood season, Mom would walk to the dock and count the steps as the water encroached and they slowly disappeared.

"I always kept one of the workers at the top of the steps at all times, watching the river," she said, reflecting back on those years of her life.

When only ten steps remained, she and my father would go into high alert mode and frantically have workers stack sandbags along the riverbank. Evacuation plans were put into affect by my father, and our staff and field workers, and we'd all move to higher ground. Though she was terrified, Mom told me years later that she would always soothe me and tell me to not worry.

On Fisher Island with my parents.

THE KING AND I

I don't remember much from those first few years of my life on the island, but one incident was recounted to me in later years so many times that it's left an indelible mark in my mind. One day, when I was just eight months old, I was playing with my mother and nanny in the living room overlooking the large veranda. (My parents always had a number of housekeepers around, which was very normal in those days.) Suddenly, the screen door flew open and servants ran into the room, very agitated.

"Madam, madam!" they cried to Mom. "There are some people outside and Master Nicholas [my father] is not here! He is out in the field."

"What should we do?" Mother asked. "Who are these people?"

"We don't know," the servants replied.

My mother hurried to the bedroom to change into a more appropriate dress, leaving the nanny and me in the living room. With the staff in a frenzy and helpless to stop the intrusion, a young man in shorts, followed by three male escorts, entered through the open door and asked to see the master of the house. The young man politely picked me up in his arms and kissed my forehead just as my mother was returning to the room, still buttoning the top of her dress. Well, that's all she had to see: A stranger holding her little boy. She grabbed me from his arms and screamed at him for his inappropriate action.

"Who are you? How dare you enter my house when my husband is not here!" she said, waiving her finger at him.

Just then, one of the escorts calmly approached Mom and said firmly: "Madam, this is King Farouk."

It took a few seconds for Mother to realize what she had done, upon which she promptly fainted right then and there. As this scene was unfolding with an embarrassed king startled by the fainted woman on the floor at his feet, my father arrived at the house after being summoned by the staff. The king greeted him with an apology.

"I'm very sorry. I should have announced myself," he said.

King Farouk's visits to the island were apparently not unusual. During the early years of his rule when he was young, Farouk traveled the country incognito, meeting his subjects and connecting with the people. Visiting the island was one of those royal expeditions. Since our house was the only residential structure on Fisher Island, the king mistook it for an office, so he did not know he was trespassing inside a private home.

For years, my maternal Grandmother Katerina would say upon reflection of the King's memorable visit that day:

"George is very special. How many boys do you know who've been kissed by a king?"

Unfortunately for Farouk, his reign did not end well. As he grew older, he became corrupt and lost touch with his people. The July 23,1952 military *coup d'etat* led by Colonel Gamal Abdel Nasser put an end to his rule. On the day of the coup, I was 16 years old and happened to be living in Alexandria. I vividly remember tanks rolling into the city and troops occupying the radio station, key ministries, government buildings and harbor. It was a classic coup, very well organized by the young officers led by Nasser. Everyone in the area was confined to their homes not knowing what the next day would bring. The first thing Nasser did was to trap Farouk into his palace and force him to abdicate and go into exile. Farouk was allowed to board his private yacht *Mahroussa* with Queen Narriman, his immediate family and close advisors. He left the country for Italy and died in Capri in 1965.

MY PARENTS AND GRANDPARENTS

Before I continue with the first leg of my lifetime journey—from tropical Fisher Island to an idyllic farm in Mariout—I'd like to share some background on my parents and grandparents, at least as much as I've been able to trace from our family tree (which I've included in Part Six).

My mom, Stella, was a very sweet and gentle woman who devoted her life to her husband and children. She had a good education growing up in Cairo. Mom attended a French school, *Le Bon Pasteur,* run by nuns. For a Greek girl in Egypt at that time, attending a French school was unusual, as Greek families typically sent their children to Greek schools. At first, Mom's father was concerned that the nuns were going to convert her to Catholicism from Greek Orthodox, but the school provided financial assistance to them and he wanted his daughter to get a first-class education. And that she did. Among other things, Mom learned to speak three languages fluently: Greek, of course, along with French and Arabic.

Later in life, when Mom came to live in America (more about that later), she added English to her list of languages. She obviously had a gift for languages because she also became conversational in Italian through her Italian aunt Marcella, who was married to her Greek Uncle Manolis. They lived in the same building as my mother and her parents while Mom was growing up in Cairo, and Stella became very close to Marcella. Even with my lifetime of travels and living in various parts of the world, my mother is still the only person I have ever known who mastered five languages. I was always really proud of her for that.

I have countless fond memories of Mom, and her cooking stands out as one of them. I can taste her Mousaka and Greek pastries like it

My mother, Stella, circa 1930.

was yesterday. She liked to cook and learned how to prepare wonderful meals from authentic recipes that my father's family brought with them from Smyrna and Constantinople, cities renowned for their cuisine.

My father, Nicholas, in the late 1920s.

As for my father's side of the family, they remained in Smyrna, Turkey until they had to flee during or after the 1922 massacre of the Greeks and Armenians by the Turks. My father, Nicholas, was probably in his twenties at that time. This is what I suspect but I can't be sure because my father never spoke about his life in Turkey. Back then, many Greeks who lived in Smyrna relocated either to Greece or south to Syria, Lebanon, and eventually to Egypt. My father's family landed in Cairo around 1922 or 1923.

To be honest, Dad and I were never close. In fact, I hardly knew him. He was smart and self-educated, but he wasn't sociable and wasn't one to open up. He didn't play with my brother Takis and me (more about him soon) or talk with us much. We never experienced the joy of listening to family stories at his knee, going to soccer games or the movies, or doing other things like fishing. I am sure Dad loved us and felt that he was taking good care of us, but I always wished that he were more affectionate. His philosophy was to leave our upbringing to Mom while he concentrated on making a good life for us.

It was only later in my life that I began to realize that Dad's earlier experiences in Smyrna had a big impact on him. He wanted very badly to provide a comfortable and safe future for his family. He was self-driven and ambitious because he had to be. He was a survivor. Like my mother, Dad spoke fluent French and Arabic in addition to his native Greek. He was a talented writer who published many stories and articles in the local papers, mostly in Greek and some in French. Despite his determination, he was never able to fulfill his true vision of building a large vineyard on the estate where we grew up (I will speak more about this in the next chapter). His dream was to achieve this goal and leave the vineyard to his sons.

The story of how my parents met is not so different from similar encounters of people who fall in love and start a life together. My father was working in a bakery when he moved to Cairo. As a young woman, my mother worked for the telephone company in Cairo, which was, I believe, owned and operated by the British. In the 1930s in Cairo, employment opportunities for young women were limited so this was a very good job for a young female. In her spare time, Mom liked to go to the movies with her friends. During one of those evenings, she noticed a man staring at her.

"Eva, every time I come to the movies," she told her friend, "somehow this guy is always looking at me. He is everywhere! I am puzzled; how does he know all my movements?"

That man was my father. Apparently, Dad knew one of Mom's friends, and this friend would give Dad a heads up on Mom's whereabouts. One day, as Mom and her girlfriends were standing in front of the cinema, Dad approached her and introduced himself in French.

"What do you do?" Mom responded to him in French.

"I'm an agronome. *Je suis un agronome.*"

Mom was impressed with Dad's manners and she couldn't help but notice that he was very handsome, with piercing green eyes and a magnetic personality.

Dad courted Mom for a while and eventually proposed. Dad was thirteen years older than Mom, which wasn't an issue for them but it was once he was introduced to her family.

"He's too old for you!" her mother (my Grandmother Katerina) announced.

My mother's reply was to the point: "I love him."

They were married in 1937. Mom was very popular and had many friends and a large family, so they were all at the wedding in Cairo to celebrate their union. There are no photos (and of course no video) of their wedding but as was more customary at that time, I found a letter dated March 7, 1953 that my father had sent to my mother 16 years after they were married and one year before his death. In it, he described with tenderness the wedding ceremony. A powerful letter to a loving wife, he titled it "Memories." Dad recalls the church ceremony with the guests arriving in horse-driven carriages, most from my mother's side. None of Dad's family attended the wedding, even though they lived in the same city. I never knew these details when my parents were alive. He reminisces about the procession of friends and relatives from the church to the train station decorated with flowers and full of young people waiting for the train to take the newlyweds to their new home on Fisher Island. His words are nostalgic, poetic, loving and optimistic, but also sad because his relatives did not attend.

Now I'd like to harken back one generation and give whatever background I have about my grandparents. I never got to meet my paternal grandparents, as they died in Smyrna before I was born. My paternal grandfather, George, was born in Smyrna, Asia Minor (Turkey) in the second half of the 19th Century. After my grandmother died, he married to a woman in Smyrna named Constantina and they had three children.

The family immigrated to Egypt as young adults. During their lives, they maintained deep roots in Greek history and culture, as did their ancestors. This Hellenistic heritage had flourished for centuries, maybe for more than millennia, in places outside Mainland Greece like Asia Minor, Russia, the Balkans, Egypt and North Africa. My father never spoke of his family and I never asked about them, so I know very little about their history and why they chose to settle in Egypt.

My mother's ancestry is not well documented, either. We know that my maternal grandmother—or, *yiayia,* as we say in Greek—Katerina Themelaros, was born in Odessa, Russia, which was under the rule of Czar Alexander III. Her father was tragically killed crossing a railroad pass when she was an infant. Katerina immigrated with her two siblings, Manolis and Athena, to the island of Leros in Greece. In the early 1900s, they relocated again to Egypt. Like my father's side of the family, they most probably did so to escape the brutal Turkish occupation of the island and due to prompting by relatives and friends who encouraged them to capitalize on the better opportunities that existed in Egypt at the time.

My Papou Yiannis in the late 1920s.

My mother's father, my Grandpa Yiannis—or Papou Yannis, as we say in Greek—was born in Sinop, Turkey, situated in the northern part of country along the Black Sea. At the time, Abdul Hamid II was the ruling sultan, as Turkey was part of the Ottoman Empire. Papou rarely spoke of his youth but he did share with me many times that when he was a small boy, he liked to go swimming every day after school in the sea.

I was very close to my Papou Yannis when I was a young lad. We had an unspoken language. He wasn't one for talking but when we were together, I could feel his warmth and love—which I craved because my father was more emotionally distant. Papou was a very mild, very kind man. He couldn't hurt a fly. He loved everybody. Papou was totally opposite from his wife, my Grandma Katerina, a strong-minded woman who ruled the household.

In Cairo in those days, there were not many cars on the streets but

Papou Yiannis and me on
Fisher Island in 1939.

Uncle Stavros, Aunt Harriette, Aunt Elefteria,
my mother and Uncle George in Cairo in 1920.

my Papou managed to have three or four accidents involving cars or motorcycles. He survived all of them. I remember him limping and his face was distorted a bit from whatever injuries he sustained, but other than that he lived a healthy life. After the third accident, Yannis was never was able to hold a job for very long. One job that Papou did manage to hold down for a while was working at a cigarette factory owned by two Greek brothers named Coutarellis. The company made cigarettes from Egyptian-grown tobacco and enjoyed a monopoly in the cigarette market in Egypt. After working there for a while, Papou quit, probably for health reasons.

A few years later, he decided to open a grocery store. Yiayia Katerina would tell me stories about the store—primarily, that customers took advantage of Papou's generosity. Everybody in the neighborhood knew him. They would come to the store to shop then tell my Papou, "Listen, I don't have any money now. Please charge it and I'll pay you later." Yannis had a very thick book with all the accounts receivable, but he seldom got paid. This went on for a number of months until they ran out of resources.

My grandmother was furious. She told me that after a few months, "we just ran out of money. We had no money. We ran out of goods and we couldn't resupply because we had no collections. Everybody owed us money and nobody paid us so we had to close the store." That was the beginning and end of Yannis' entrepreneurial venture.

Papou mostly spent his spare time going to the kafenio, the neighborhood coffee shop. This is where the local men gathered to play backgammon, drink coffee and engage in lively and loud discussions, mainly involving politics. I remember Papou with his cane and straw hat leaving the house for the shop, while my grandmother complained about his not making enough money and how she had to shoulder the responsibility all by herself to raise five children.

Aunt Artemis and her mother, Constantina,
in Cairo circa 1939.

I loved my Papou. He was my best friend. I lived with my grand-parents in Alexandria during my last two years of high school (I will share later how and why that came to be) and my room was next to Papou's room. He would make me Greek coffee and sit silently next to me, watching me study and do my homework. He was very proud of me. Sometimes he would ask me:

"How can all these books, all these words fit in your brain? I don't understand that. Tell me."

He couldn't fathom how I could read so many books for so many hours, and remember what I had read. But he was smart in his own way, too. He taught me how to play backgammon and I became a good player because of him.

My Papou told me very little about his youth. I know that one day when he was still young, his parents left Sinop with him and his and brother, Christos, for Egypt. His third younger brother, Dimitris, decided to stay behind in Sinop. (His amazing experience of surviving the Turkish massacre of the Greeks is detailed in my cousin John Barbas' story in Part Five.) Grandpa Yiannis never told me the circumstances or reasons why they left their home, or when. I regret that I never thought to ask him about his life when we lived together in Alexandria, or later when I was studying in America, and before he died in Alexandria in 1960. My theory is that they left because of the persecution of Greeks and Armenians by the Turks. At that time (the early 1900s), Egypt was under the rule of the progressive and pro-European Mohamed Ali Dynasty and later under British protection and was therefore a safe place for displaced Europeans to seek new homes and a fresh start with their families.

A TWO-YEAR-OLD EVZONAS

I'd like to share a couple of details about my extended family in Egypt, and one memorable story from when I was just two years old. My mother, Stella, had four siblings: Uncle George, Uncle Stavros (Steve), Aunt Elefteria (Liberty) and Aunt Harriette. I knew all of them. In fact, I was very close to all of my aunts and uncles. I was the first child born into the family and none of these uncles and aunts were married with children yet (that came later), so I was doted on by everyone, the sole recipient of their love, smiles, hugs and, of course, toys. They spoiled me and I loved it.

Dressed in my Evzonas uniform in Cairo 1941.

After they escaped the Turkish genocide in the early 1920s, my father's stepmother, Constantina, and his half-sister, Artemis, settled in Cairo. That's where I remember them and where I visited them when I was a child, but we were not close. My grandparents from my father's side were all deceased when I was born, and with the exception of Artemis, I knew very little about my father's siblings because they had also died before I was born. The name of my Aunt Artemis always fascinated me. In Greek mythology, Artemis is the goddess of the hunt and the nat-

Thirteen years later, in 1954, standing with my parents and brother Takis in front of the Greek Parliament in Athens with elite Evzones soldiers guarding the tomb of the unknown soldier.

ural environment. True to the nature of this Greek goddess, Aunt Artemis was a very beautiful woman: blonde, blue eyes, stunning. She was married to an Egyptian Christian by the name of William. I remember him very well. He was tall and handsome.

Growing up, I was told a lot of stories about William and Artemis' very beautiful wedding. I vaguely recall some photographs of that day, and the following details were recounted to me when I was older, as I was only two years old and have no recollection of them. For the ceremony, my mother dressed me in a traditional Greek warrior's uniform called the Evzones costume. Even today, you can see these impressive soldiers in Athens standing at attention in front of the Parliament building, guarding the tomb of the unknown soldier. They're very sharp looking, with white kilts and black vests.

The wedding ceremony took place in a Greek Orthodox Cathedral in Cairo. After the church service, I rode with the newlyweds in a six-horse-driven carriage, like royalty. As the carriage traveled through the streets of Cairo, I stood next to the driver waving the Greek flag. We drove through the main square and boulevards, with bystanders applauding and sending best wishes to the bride and groom. It was a moment of glory for a little boy at his aunt's "royal" wedding, dressed as an Evzonas and proudly waving the colors of his homeland.

2

A Vineyard in the Desert

"Who would buy farmland in the desert?"

My outspoken Grandmother Katerina thought that my father had lost his mind when he announced his intentions to buy a farm situated 70 kilometers southwest of Alexandria, at the edge of the Western Sahara. The land was located in an underdeveloped area called Mariout—not far from Masrah Matrouh and Tobruk, sites where significant battles took place during World War II. A 10-kilometer drive outside these towns would land you right in the middle of an isolated desert.

"Your husband has a good job, and he makes good money," Grandma prodded Mom. "Why he wants to risk all that by buying land in the desert? I don't know!"

Dad had a vision of owning and running a prosperous vineyard. So when I was two years old, our family moved from Fisher Island to Mariout, some 200 miles west of Cairo. Along with my mother and his financing partner Mourafetlis, a rich Greek businessman from Cairo, they bought 600 acres in the western frontier near the largest vineyard in Egypt owned by Nestor Gianaclis, a visionary Greek businessman who lived in Egypt. The story of how we came to acquire the farm speaks to my father's ingenuity and foresight.

My father's choice to buy land in the region of Mariout, near Gianaclis' eponymous vineyards, was based on Gianaclis' success. He'd
come to Egypt in the early 1900s from a poor family in Greece seeking
opportunity and a better future, and became very interested in the area
of Mariout, which covers several hundred miles south of the Alexan-
dria-to-Tripoli coastline.

Gianaclis sought out this region because of its illustrious history and
deep Greek roots. Mariout is the Arabic translation of the Greek Mareo-
tis. More than 2,000 years ago, the Ptolemaic Dynasty governed Egypt.
They were Greek Macedonians, successors of Alexander the Great, who
after Alexander's death, came to Egypt and styled themselves pharaohs.
Cleopatra was the last Ptolemi Pharaoh Queen from that dynasty and
after her death Egypt became a Roman province. It would not become
independent until the 20th Century. Under the Ptolemies' rule, wealthy
aristocracy had built imposing homes on the shores of Lake Mariout.
The rich soil and perfect weather provided the ideal conditions to grow
grapes and develop large vineyards. Their wines were famous well beyond the borders of Mariout and even Egypt.

Gianaclis was intrigued by Mariout's history but he also saw the
vast potential of the region. He began buying land cheap and by the
1930s had acquired 30,000 acres of desert, putting his capital and reputation on the line. Over a period of thirty years, he developed and owned
the largest vineyard in Egypt and became a very rich man.

My father often talked about Gianaclis and it inspired me to write
the following article in 1950 when I was in seventh grade. It was published in the school's monthly newspaper. For a seventh grader, I think
my Greek writing was very good, but more significantly, the description
of our lives at the farm brought my narrative to life. Of course, I've
translated it here from the Greek (also included below):

From the Farm: The Harvest in Egypt

When Nestor Gianaclis (a wealthy Greek businessman living in Egypt) decided to grow vines in the area of Abu Matamir in Mariout, he selected this area based on its history, which dates back to ancient times. This is where the successors of Alexander the Great, the Ptolemies, grew grapes and the wealthy people at the time built lavish homes in the middle of vineyards, on the shores of Lake Mariout. In modern times, Greek businessmen realized the potential of the area and bought land and developed the most famous and vineyards in Egypt.

My brother and I grew up in our father's small vineyard adjacent to the much larger Gianaclis estate. We spent our childhood here in a happy, carefree environment surrounded by vineyards and nature. In the summer, after sunrise, the sun would dry the grapes from the mist of the night. Young Bedouin girls would then harvest the golden grapes, and load them on a horse-driven carriage to be taken to the warehouse to be cleaned and packed in boxes before transported to markets in cities in Egypt.

Ὁ τρυγητὸς στὴν Αἴγυπτο

"Οταν ὁ ἀείμνηστος Νέστωρ Τσανακλῆς ἀνέλαβε τὴν πρωτοβουλίαν νὰ καλλιεργήσῃ ἀμπελῶνας στὴν ξακουστὴν περιφέρειαν τοῦ "Αμπου - Ματαμὶρ στὸ Μαριοὺτ ἐβασίσθηκε στὴ παληὰ Πτολεμαϊκὴ ἐποχὴ ποὺ τ' ἀμπέλι εὐδοκιμοῦσε ἐξαιρετικὰ στὴν θαυμαστὴ αὐτὴ περιφέρεια τοῦ Μαριούτ. Λέγουν μάλιστα πὼς στὶς ὄχθες τῆς Μαρεώτιδος λίμνης ἦσαν ἐγκατεστημένοι σὲ ὡραῖες ἐπαύλεις οἱ πλούσιοι τῆς ἐπο-

χῆς ἐκείνης, μὲ τοὺς ἀπεράντους ἀμπελῶνες ποὺ τὰ κρασιά τους φημισμένα κι' αὐτὰ εὔφραιναν ὅλους.

Καὶ ἄρχισε τὸ φύτευμα τῶν ἀμπελιῶν ποὺ ἔγινε μιὰ μεγάλη ἑλληνικὴ ἐπιχείρησι γεωργικὴ βιομηχανικὴ μὲ τὲς ἀπέραντες κάβες τῶν κρασιῶν τους καὶ τὰς ἀπεράντους ἐκτάσεις τῶν ἀμπελώνων.

— Σ' ἕνα τέτοιο περιβάλλον μεγαλώσαμε ἐγὼ καὶ ὁ ἀδελφός μου στὸ μικρὸ πατρικό μας κτῆμα, σ' αὐτὸ γνώρισα τὴν παιδικὴ χαρὰ τῆς ζωῆς τῆς ὑπαίθρου, ξεγνοιαστα χρόνια ἐλεύθερα, χαρούμενα, μέσ' τοὺς ἀμπελῶνες μὲ τὰ χρυσαφένια τσαμπιά τους.

Μετὰ τὴν ἀνατολὴ τοῦ ἡλίου κι' ὅταν οἱ θερμὲς ἀκτῖνες του, ἐστέγνωναν τὰ μουσκεμένα τσαμπιὰ ἀπὸ τὴν ὁλόνυκτη ὑγρασία βεδουΐνες μὲ τὰ πανέρια στὸ κεφάλι γιομάτα σταφύλια τὰ μεταφέρουν στὸ ὑπόστεγο.

'Εκεῖμέσα ἄλλες βεδουΐνες μὲ μικρὰ ψαλίδια στὸ χέρι καθαρίζουν τὰ τσαμπιὰ ἀπὸ τὶς ἄγουρες ἢ σάπιες ρόγες.

"Υστερα συσκευάστριες μὲ ἐπιδέξια τέχνη γιομίζουν τὰ καφάσια ποὺ θὰ ταξιδεύσουν σ' ὅλες τὶς πόλεις τῆς Αἰγύπτου.

Καὶ τώρα ποὺ τὴν ξεγνοιασιὰ τῆς ὑπαίθρου τὴν διεδέχθησαν τὰ μαθήματα, μὲ λαχτάρα περιμένομε τὶς παύσεις γιὰ νὰ πᾶμε στὸν τόπον ποὺ πάντα μᾶς τραβᾶ κοντά του.

ΓΕΩΡΓ. Ν. ΘΕΟΤΟΚΑΤΟΣ

(Α'.)

Original Greek text of my article "From the Farm."

Egypt in those days was open and friendly towards all European settlers who were allowed to live there, buy land and own businesses with no restrictions. Many of the Europeans who came to Egypt were displaced people seeking safety and homes for their families; others sought opportunities to acquire wealth. They became landowners and businessmen. They built factories and schools and hospitals. They were educated and brought with them talent, determination, a good work ethic and capital. They worked hard and became successful.

My father worked very hard to create such a beautiful place in the middle of nowhere. It took him 14 years to bring this beautiful vineyard to its fullest fruition and we faced many hardships along the way. We had no electricity, no running water, no refrigerator. The nearest village was miles away, reachable only on unpaved roads, which made it impossible to drive anywhere when the rains came. Like Fisher Island, being in the remote desert was very difficult for our mom because she had to raise two kids with no facilities or family support, although we did have a lot of domestic help.

*On the farm in Mariout on my ninth birthday (1947)
with Takis, Bedouin workers and Mom.*

The farm was located in a region where Bedouin tribes lived and grazed their goats, so these nomadic tribes provided the workforce for our farm. At the peak of the season, we had a couple hundred workers on the land. Mostly, we produced grapes for table consumption, but we also grew orchard trees: peaches, apples, prunes and pears. To ensure biodiversity, we added seasonal crops like wheat, corn and cotton.

A couple of years after Dad purchased the land, the Egyptian government enlarged and dredged a small irrigation canal, which happened to pass directly in front of our property. After another couple of years, Egypt implemented ambitious development plans by reclaiming the Western Sahara border with irrigation projects, thus making more farmland available. Infrastructure projects like roads were gradually put in thus making the transportation of goods easier and more cost effective.

After all that came to pass, no one—not even my grandmother—was making fun of my father anymore for buying real estate in the dry lands. His vision for the region's potential was literally springing to life. Dad had developed a remarkable vineyard and fruitful business enterprise—yes, smack in the middle of the desert.

FUN ON THE FARM

When I think of my childhood from age six to eighteen, my mind immediately reflects back on the fourteen years that we owned this farm. Though we spent only our summer months there (except for Dad, who lived there year round), the farm was the centerpiece of my life and my brother Takis' life. The rest of the year, we went to school near our home in Alexandria.

From these precious summers of our youth, my brother and I learned at a very early age how to caretake the land, the vines and trees, and the animals. It's where we worked and played together, just the two of us. Takis (Chris) is two years younger than me and we have different personalities, but were always very close and still are. Perhaps it's because we really only had each other growing up. As kids, we had school friends in Alexandria but during the summer months on the farm we didn't have many choices of playmates, as there were no other families or children nearby; so we had each other to play and fight with and do all the things that little boys do. Being the older brother, I was expected to look after Takis, which I took very seriously then and also now.

During the summers on the farm, we mostly worked but as children, we always found things to do that gave us pleasure. We didn't have toys and there were no stores around like you have today, so we had to be creative. We made our own toys using clay. One of the workers at the farm, Younis, was very good with his hands and he showed us how to make clay models and sculptures. Since he was the caretaker of the stable and the animals, most of our figures were of miniature animals, particularly cows, horses, dogs, donkeys and buffaloes. We'd build them in all sizes then put them in the oven to bake for half an hour until they hardened. We kept these toy animals all around the house. It was the biggest game collection we'd ever had.

Takis and I improvised in other ways, too, when it came to entertaining ourselves. One of our favorite things to do was build and fly kites. We became very good at it. I was the mastermind and chief engineer, and he was my assistant and chief architect. We started out experimenting with building small kites from bamboo and colorful paper of blue and white (to represent the Greek flag). For glue, we used a pasty mixture of flour and water, testing various proportions until we got the right consistency and results. Our first kites were simple to build and easy to fly. They all had the same rectangular shape and a long, flowing tail. As we gained experience and confidence, we progressed to making bigger and bigger and bigger models.

Our kite-building pursuits culminated in us constructing the ultimate flying machine. I don't remember the dimensions it must have been six or seven feet high and five feet wide. The day finally came to launch our creation. We took to an open field to set it free. Our excitement and anticipation grew as we slid the rope through our fingers and watched this beautiful beast ascend rapidly and anxiously towards the sky.

It was magnificent! Off it went up, up, up. We didn't anticipate the power of this kite against the wind. It began to pull us with tenacity, as if to say, "Eh, you guys, I want to be truly free! Let go of the rope!" Our struggle became like fishermen reeling in the big one. Takis and I had to hold the line with both hands to keep it under our control. We kept feeding the line out, which only made the kite fly higher and higher, almost reaching the clouds. Then I did something I probably shouldn't have done. The air blew my hat away and I told Takis I wanted to retrieve it.

"Would you hold the line for one minute?" I asked, letting go of the rope and leaving him to fly the kite solo.

A few seconds later after getting my hat, I looked up and to my horror Takis was off the ground, holding onto the line for dear life and desperately trying to gain control of the kite as it lifted him up. I panicked and attempted to pull him back down but I wasn't strong enough. I screamed and screamed, and a few of the farm hands working nearby rushed to the scene. Together, we managed to pull Takis to the ground. I'm making it sound dramatic because, at the time, it was to us, but in reality, the kite dragged Takis maybe at least ten feet and he was just a few inches airborne.

Takis and I also loved spending time with the many animals we had on the farm, including three horses, five donkeys, three buffalos, chickens, geese, pigs and five dogs. Today, I know that my grandkids love animals too (more about that in Part Four), so maybe the farmer in me has been handed down to them.

The dogs were mainly guard dogs, protecting us from people who would try to steal our crops. They mostly lived in their doghouse outside, but they were our best friends and constant companions. Peggy was the alpha female and was in control of the rest of the pack all the time. Originally a city dog, our friends in Alexandria had gotten her when she was puppy; later on, they could not keep her in their apartment any longer and they asked if we would adopt her. We were happy to take Peggy to the farm. In the beginning, she was not friendly but slowly she became very protective of us and served her role very well.

One of the other canines, Major, had only one eye. I don't remember how we got him but I know he lost that eye in a fight with another dog, so he was tough. We also had a black German Shepherd. Leon was true to his breed: strong, obedient, smart and courageous. Wherever we went, he and the other dogs were always with us, even when we went hunting or just for a walk.

I also loved caretaking the horses on the farm although they always intimidated me. I was not afraid of them but I was not at ease with the more aggressive types. I had my own horse named Jamila—Arabic for "beautiful"—and she sure was. Jamila was reddish-brown with a golden tail, small in size with a small head so she probably had some Arabian horse blood in her. She was very fast, and she liked to eat carrots and sugar. The first thing that she would do in the morning when the guys from the stable would bring her to the house for me to ride was to put her mouth into my pocket. She knew that I always had a sugar cube in one pocket and carrots in another. In the winters, when I was away at school in Alexandria, I missed my dogs and my horse for months on end.

As far back as I can remember, I've always had an affinity for birds. On the farm, I raised pigeons. I had a large collection of various breeds: small ones, big ones, white and red and black. I trained these feathered creatures to fly in formation using flags, one in each hand; I'd wave the red one in my right hand and the white flag on the left hand at different sequences, giving the pigeons flying above me clues about how and where to fly. Some were fast and some were slow. Others would fly away or would steal other pigeons. These were birds that would actually persuade other pigeons to fly back with them into our coup. We nicknamed them "the thieves." These small white pigeons had this ability to bring pigeons belonging to other people back with them. Other people who also had pigeons knew that we had these "thief" pigeons, so they had their own, as well. An ongoing war ensued about who was going to steal more pigeons from the other person. Most of the time, to be honest, we never knew where the stolen pigeons came from.

EARLY WORK LESSONS

Life on the farm was not all fun and games, however; in fact, Takis and I had specific chores, work assignments and responsibilities assigned to us by our father and we took them all very seriously. Dad treated us like adults and expected us to behave responsibly and discharge our duties with diligence.

My main responsibility during the harvest period—from late July until the grape harvest ended in September—was to supervise the assembly line and packaging of the freshly harvested grapes into boxes to be shipped to the market. This all took place in the huge warehouse that served as our collection center. The workers, mostly young girls, would handpick grapes from the vines. In the field, the collected grapes would then be loaded onto a horse-driven flatbed carriage and taken to the central collection center to be prepared for shipping. Inside the collection center were several Pi-shaped tables. Each table had four girls sitting on each side to handle the grapes; a packer stood in the middle. The girls used small scissors to remove any rotten pieces and clean the grapes before placing them on the table. The packers would then pick up the cleaned grapes and place them in boxes. At the end of the day, all boxes would be loaded onto a truck and taken to the markets in Alexandria to be sold.

At the peak of harvest season and counting all the staff, we employed anywhere from 50 to 75 people, so I was really kind of the big honcho. The workers called me Mr. George. For a young boy, having this responsibility was a big deal. I started doing this at the age of twelve and my responsibilities increased as I grew older. My biggest challenge was ensuring that the work got done in an environment that was fair for all the employees. In those days, there was no such thing as unions or worker's rights, but I had a strong desire that we had to be fair with our employees. They were poor, uneducated, nomadic people living a very basic existence. They had no health facilities, no schools. They all came to work for us from the surrounding villages or hamlets. We paid a lot of attention to our workers and took care of them. We wanted them to feel like they belonged and that they could trust us.

I was pretty much successful in this endeavor over my years in the warehouse. This experience, as it turned out, helped me greatly later in life. It formed a foundation for my managerial skills, which I would need in my career and at home as an adult. It helped me to truly understand people.

I also learned the power of money. My father used to pay me a few piasters a day (less than one dollar), a nominal amount in today's standards but good money in those days. As I had no outlets for spending this money during the summer months on the farm, I saved all of it. Those savings played a big role in shaping my lifestyle during the winters back in Alexandria. I was known as the rich kid on the block. I had disposable income and sometimes even lent it to people who did not have money or who were going through difficult times. This gave me a sense of power and a taste of what money could do. Takis earned his own money and so he learned these things, as well.

As the warehouse supervisor, another one of my biggest challenges was how to discipline somebody who wasn't doing a good job. There I was, a boy, trying to reprimand a rough, 45-year-old Bedouin who used to come to work with his gun on his back. He'd park his gun outside the warehouse then go to work. My father was always worried about that gun sitting there. So I had to maintain an aura of authority without being childish or confrontational or dangerous. I had a natural desire to always strike a balance, to know how far to push. There was a line that I was always aware not to cross. My skills were tested more than a few times.

One time was when one of the workers wasn't doing his job properly. I would tell him to do something and he would ignore me. The way I addressed the issue was to always fall back on tribal law and customs. In difficult cases, like this one, I would talk to the elder person of the tribe or group working on our land. Usually these people were the foremen on our farm. We had two people with such status. One was Abdullah, a handsome man with a very light complexion, blondish hair and a big mustache. The other person with a great deal of authority and influence was Faiza, a beautiful single woman in her early thirties. Faiza was really the boss on the farm, overshadowing everyone else. It was unusual for a woman to have authority, particularly in those days. Faiza was ahead of the women's liberation movement by at least sixty years. She would have made Gloria Steinem proud.

So when my father was away traveling, I would go and talk to the tribe leader in charge.

"Look, we got a problem here, what do we do?" I would ask.

By doing that, I learned early in life that when you bring people into the decision-making process and make them part of the resolution, you create solutions more easily. Most of the time, but not always, I was able to work out any problems by bringing these elders into the picture.

GUNSLINGERS IN OUR MIDST

Our farmland may have been remote but we had our share of commotion from time to time. One night when my father was away and we were sleeping, we heard gunfire. The dogs were barking and we heard our guards shooting their rifles (yes, we had guards). Was there an intruder? My mother and I sprung awake and went out to the veranda to see what was going on. Thieves had cut the fence. They were stealing our grapes and loading them into their trucks.

Mom wanted to go out and assess the situation. She told me to stay in the house with Takis, who slept through the whole ordeal. She walked alone in the pitch black of night to where the trouble was. I worried that she was doing this. I was only twelve and very scared—for myself, for my mom, for the situation. For many years after the incident, I felt guilt for not being with her. In retrospect, her decision to leave the house and her children alone and venture in the middle of the night into a gunfire zone was a mistake. She could have been killed or injured. In fact, for months after the incident, she suffered from severe headaches and neck problems that doctors attributed to stress and her being out in the cold weather that night.

A few years later, we experienced another violent situation at the farm with a man who gave us a lot of trouble. His name was Shafik and I will never forget him. This bandit was going around terrorizing people. He was a real bad guy, a character of the wild, wild American West, a real outlaw. Shafik may have even watched American movies and copy-catted the gunslingers of the old frontier. He covered his face with a black mask and carried a vintage shotgun. Shafik would hijack cars on the road and rob the passengers at gunpoint. Sometimes he would beat his victims but he never killed anyone. He would terrorize my mother by standing in front of our house when she was sitting in the veranda watching us play, or he would take his shotgun and aim it towards my father as he walked down the road while returning home. A few minutes later, he would laugh and walk away. No one dared to stop him or do anything about it for fear of retribution.

I remember one time when we had a friend paying us a visit. Vasilis, a Greek fellow who worked across the river on another farm, came to have lunch with us. After lunch, he left to walk back to his farm. Then, twenty minutes later, we saw him running back, bleeding, with a big gash on his head and his face all cut up. Apparently, Shafik had been waiting for him outside the gate. He beat him up and took his watch, his shoes and the couple of pounds (the local currency) that he had in his pocket.

A few months after this incident with Vasilis, we returned to the farm from Alexandria and found that our house had been broken into and most of our personal belongings were gone. Thieves had broken through the thick wall in the back of the house and entered. We questioned our guards and they swore they didn't see anything. We all knew who the culprit was; of course, it was Shafik. Earlier he had asked my father for "protection money" but my father ignored him. This robbery was his answer. We had to negotiate with him a buyback price to have him return all of our personal belongings except a few shirts that he liked and kept.

After a while, Shafik the bandit became too much of a nuisance when he began to antagonize the rich landowners in the area. He made a lot of enemies and influential people started to complain. Finally, a delegation of them went to see the state governor.

"Look, this has to stop," they demanded.

Soon thereafter, one early morning, army units (not police) drove into Shafik's village and rounded up all the women and took them to the police station. They told the elders of the tribe that unless this guy is brought to the police station soon, the governor could not guarantee the safety of the women. Within two days, his own people caught him and took him to the police station, and that was the end of him. We never saw or heard of Shafik again. Tribal law was applied again in a brutal way to solve a local security problem. And so our summers went—supervising the grape pickers, taking care of the crops and animals, and warding off bandits and thieves. As I was growing stronger and taller, and my brother was too, my father's vision was very simple and his goal was clear: Takis and I would stay on the farm and buy more land when we were of age. Since Egypt was our home, upon graduation from high school, Dad expected that we would both attend the local university, study agriculture then return to Mariout to work the land, as we had all those summers of our youth. Our father, however, never shared his views about our future with my brother and me. We were not given the opportunity to say what we really wanted to do with our lives. It was assumed that our future was linked to the farm. Period.

There was only one glitch in my father's dream. My vision was different: I wanted to live in America. I believe that my mother had a different version of future reality, as well: She wanted to see her children become scientists, businessmen or engineers, not farmers. She wanted a better life for her children than the one she had been living in remote locations away from civilization.

Little did I know that during my high school years, my life would be altered in an emotionally traumatic way and I would take another direction than our father had planned for me and my brother altogether.

3

Carefree in Alexandria

I t was a normal Friday morning in March 1954 in Ibrahimia, a quaint
neighborhood outside the city hub of Alexandria where many ethnic
groups lived, mainly Greeks. I woke up early and got dressed for school.
I was a sophomore in high school and busy with schoolwork and social
activities. The weather outside was perfect: a spring day in Alexandria,
sunny and mild, a slight breeze blowing in off the sea. Down in our tiny
kitchen, Takis and I quickly ate the delicious breakfast that our mother
had prepared as we discussed the activities ahead of us that day and
my father's visit from the farm the next day. At eight o'clock, as usual,
we left the house and walked fifteen minutes to the tram station. These
cable cars were the standard way of transport in Alexandria at that time,
and probably still are today.

The tram station was crowded with youngsters like us waiting to
board the train for school. There were several foreign schools of different nationalities along the rail of the tram. I boarded and at the next stop
I saw my girlfriend, Olga, waiting in her usual spot. I waved and sig-
naled for her to join me on board. The next stop was where the French
school Lycée Français was located; all the French-speaking students
disembarked. The following station was the English school Saint Mark,

so all the English-speaking students jumped off. The well known Don Bosco, an Italian vocational school, and Sacred Heart, the English girl's school followed. And the final two stops, Mazarita and Sauter, covered the biggest complex of foreign schools where all Greek schools and the Greek stadium where assembled. The remaining passengers in the tram, mostly Greek students (myself included), got off the tram and walked to our respective buildings and classrooms.

The Greek school complex consisted of several buildings spread over seventy acres of land. The educational facilities were organized by gender and vocation. Boys and girls went to separate schools. Classics, Science and Commercial schools were each housed in their own buildings. There was also an orphanage on the grounds, an enclosed gym and the famous Enosis Stadium. Academic standards were very intense. In addition to the core courses of mathematics, physics, chemistry, history and the classics, we were required to take Arabic three times a week, as well as French and English. The basic principle of the school was to assign lots of homework each day.

The most famous institution in this huge complex of buildings was Averofio High School, built in 1886 in a classic architectural style from private donations by the great benefactor George Averoff. It became famous for its rich library, science museum and Greek programs. It was a tough, competitive school. Most of my classmates went on to achieve prominent professional careers in engineering, medicine, science and business, mostly in Greece where they relocated after the purge of foreign nationals by Nasser in the 1960s. A few graduates like my brother and me immigrated to America, Australia and Europe.

HAPPY DAYS

Life in Alexandria in those days was good and happy. As youngsters, we enjoyed the beaches and many of the typical things that boys do. In those days, the cinema was the centerpiece of our entertainment. My friends and I loved going to the movies and there were about ten cinemas in

Alexandria. Most were modern luxurious facilities with American and French names like Cinema Metro, Odeon, Rialto, Gaitee and The Rex. They showed the latest releases of American films, some French and a few Egyptian.

We would sink into the comfortable cinema seats and get totally lost in the make believe world of Hollywood. This was the height of the 1950s, when America was extending its image and influence all over the globe. It was an era when America was at its top, experiencing its halcyon days. We watched with intense admiration and some envy about American drive-ins and how families had television sets in their homes (these things were not available in Egypt in those days). Popular singers like Elvis Presley and Bill Haley brought rock n' roll and dances like "The Twist" into our lives. Glamorous movie stars like Grace Kelly, Marilyn Monroe, James Dean and others kept our small provincial minds mesmerized as we watched the big screen thousands of miles away, with cool kids and sporty cars that we so much envied and loved.

I had my favorite shows and movies, of course. The weekly Zorro series played at the Metropolitan Cinema located on Corniche by the Sea. We would go to see the main feature, but beforehand was a half-hour segment of Zorro, with a different episode every week. Zorro, the masked man who carried a sword, was a good guy always doing valiant things and chasing villains. And he always won. In a way, Zorro was my hero, always fighting for the right causes and helping people in need.

Sports and athletic competitions were also a key part in our young lives. In particular, I loved to watch and play basketball. In high school, I played forward position on the varsity team. I was good at it. Sixty years later, I still remember the best game of my life. We were playing in an intra-school championship and many people had come to the game. It was a nice afternoon, typical of Alexandria weather in the spring. We were the underdog team with a slim chance to win, but I felt confident and soon began to score one basket after another. I was on fire. My teammates kept passing the ball to me and I kept finding the basket no matter how many players from the other team were on top of me. We won! I think the score was 62 to 58. I don't remember exactly, but I think I scored 40 points out of the 62 total. The takeaway here is that when you feel in the zone, you know it and take it all the way. What a feeling! There have been other instances in my life when this same "in the zone" experience has made me more resolute in critical situations and confident to take chances and make crucial decisions when needed.

Aside from movies and sports, one of our favorite ways to enjoy good, clean fun was to have parties at someone's home. These parties were a venue to bring boys and girls together and dance, and occasionally have a cigarette—which, by the way, was taboo in that society. There were no alcoholic drinks available, as they were too expensive and we weren't allowed to have them on the premises. Occasionally, however, someone would sneak in a bottle or two of cheap wine but we always drank in moderation. I don't remember ever seeing anybody drunk. We had these house parties almost every weekend.

On one particular Friday afternoon, I went home to rest and do most of my homework for next week since I had a very busy social schedule lined up for the weekend. That night, my friend Costas had organized a party at his house. Costas knew a guy (I don't recall his name) who had a portable 78 rpm record player and owned many records, mostly American songs. This guy's main interest was to bring his records to parties for a small fee and play them while everybody danced. I don't recall ever seeing him dancing or socializing with a girl. He was happy sitting in the corner playing his records and sipping a drink, and we were happy that he was there with his records, giving us the opportunity to dance and enjoy listening to Dean Martin, Johnny Mathis, Harry Belafonte, Bill Hailey, Pat Boone, Frankie Laine, Patti Page and many others. I also liked Latin music, particularly Argentinian tangos, and this guy played records of famous tango singers like Carlos Cardel (the king of the tango), Julio Sosul and others. I was—and still am, to a lesser extent—an excellent tango dancer. And finally he had a complete collection of old Greek favorites and modern Greek music. Looking back, I think we were very fortunate to know this guy. You could say that he was our private DJ.

Sometimes at the end of these evenings, after our house parties, we would walk home and stop at some girl's house in the early hours of the morning and sing songs under her window. It was a classic serenade, with the often outcome being some angry father waking up and screaming through the window at us to go home . . . or else! At that point, the group would break up and soon find our way home, happy to be young and experiencing feelings of friendship and love.

Throughout my life, I've been very blessed to have good friends, many of whom I've known since my school days. After more than fifty years removed from my high school graduation, I still meet with these friends during my visits to Athens. Unfortunately, as we get older and people pass or relocate, the circle of friends is diminishing. I am also fortunate to enjoy a small circle of friends who live in the New York area, some of them dating back to our college days. We meet as often as we can, enjoying each other's company and reminiscing about the old days—which is, of course, the point of this entire book.

SHOCK WAVES

Some things, however, are not so easy to reflect back upon. One evening when I was sixteen years old, we were all out visiting my grandparents who lived fifteen minutes from our house—Dad, Mom, Takis and me. We'd had a lovely dinner with Papou and Yiayia and afterwards, my parents and Takis left to go home. I stayed to visit longer and decided to sleep over.

The stark ringing of the doorbell at two o'clock in the morning roused us from sleep. My Papou opened the door and I heard our family friend, Michael, talking in a faint voice.

"Nicholas is gone," he said through tears to Papou. "He's gone. Nicholas is gone."

I don't remember how I got back to our house but when I did, I found Mother and Takis in a state of shock. We embraced and cried together in disbelief. How could this be? Dad was seemingly a very healthy man, strong and still in his fifties. His passing was so sudden, probably the result of a stroke, and it didn't seem real. Throughout the night, lots of people came to the house: the doctor, neighbors, friends. We lived in a tight community where friends were always there in times of need. They all mourned with us.

Needless to say, my father's death changed our lives forever. It created huge unforeseen challenges for us all and left important decisions to be made that affected the course of our lives. Mom was burdened with handling all business related to the farm and shouldering related debts. She considered selling but the elders in my family—my uncles and their investment partner—made the decision to not liquidate the farm. They put pressure on Mom to keep it, saying that she and Takis should manage it. This necessitated Mom making the difficult decision to pull my brother out of school at the age of fourteen. I thought this was a terrible decision and unfair to my brother. My mother had no other viable option but to accept the decision to manage the farm with Takis.

"This is nonsense." I said in response to this decision. "Don't do that! Just liquidate the farm and let the partner worry about it."
I voiced my objections but the adults in the family were only concerned with how we were going to survive. They insisted that I finish my last year of high school. I went to live with my grandparents for two years in Alexandria then graduated from Averofio High School in 1956.

In the meantime, Mom's younger sister, Harriette, had gone to America, married there and became an American citizen. The couple did not have any children and I was always close to this aunt. As events in Egypt worsened under Nasser around the time of my high school graduation, Aunt Harriette invited me to come to America to study at the university. This was the silver lining in an otherwise dark time in my life. Finally, my dream might be coming true: studying in America. I applied to several colleges and was accepted at New York University's School of Engineering. I began plans to leave immediately after graduation but my plan was thwarted by one more shock wave.

NASSER'S REVOLUTION

That same year, Gamal Abdel Nasser nationalized the Suez Canal. Israel, France and Britain retaliated by declaring war on Egypt. The combined armies of the three countries crossed the Suez Canal and swiftly began marching towards Cairo. President Eisenhower, however, intervened and stopped the joined forces. He forced them to retreat to the Sinai Peninsula thus saving Nasser from defeat and humiliation. The irony is that American intervention allowed Nasser to expand his social revolution not only in Egypt but in the neighboring Arab countries of Syria, Sudan and Yemen. He was then free to aggressively continue his socialist ideas and anti-American policies for the next decade.

The impact of these events on my plans to relocate to the United States was significant. New travel restrictions blocked me from leaving Egypt, and I didn't want to leave my mother alone while the hostilities were going on. So I postponed my departure for one year to evaluate the situation, decide what to do and how to do it, and gather the monetary resources I needed. I went up to the farm and worked there for a while. Egypt was obviously going through fundamental social and political upheaval. After the Suez crisis, the government nationalized all Jewish, French and English interests, banks, properties and deported Jewish, English and French nationals overnight. They gave them 24 hours to leave the country even though most of them were born there.

At the beginning, Nasser recognized the Greek contribution to the safe operation of the canal and the Greeks were spared. Hundreds of them from the small island of Kastellorizo had immigrated to Egypt many years before and worked for the French and English who were administering the operation of the Suez Canal before the war. They held critical jobs as captains and pilots running the tugs and moving the ships through the canal. (A vessel going through the canal has to have a pilot to navigate it during the passage.) During the crisis, Nasser personally asked this group of Greeks who lived in Suez and the small town of Ismailia along the canal to stay on and help him run the canal. The boycott by the warring European and Jewish parties failed, largely because during the crisis, the Greek pilots continued navigating ships through the Suez Canal thus enabling Egypt to collect critical revenues and survive.

Nasser personally assured the Greek community that because of their critical support during the crisis, he was not going to harm them.

Unfortunately, often promises that politicians make are forgotten. A few years later, Nasser began to indirectly purge the remaining Europeans left in the country, including the Greeks. He passed laws prohibiting non-Egyptian citizens from finding employment or owning a business. If you were not Muslim, you couldn't work. Slowly but steadily, Nasser began to choke down on all foreign enterprises, factories and land owners.

Eventually, the Nasser agrarian reform and nationalization laws trickled down to a very personal level: My family began to seriously consider leaving Egypt and seeking home elsewhere. Once again, this generation of my ancestors had to grapple with immigrating for their very survival. History was repeating itself. In the end, we lost our beloved farm as all properties owned by foreign and wealthy Egyptians were nationalized. The very thing that my family fought so hard to save was now gone. These were very difficult times for my family. In a short period of fourteen years, from when my father bought the land to building it up to a successful farming operation, we went from nothing to everything then back to nothing.

By the mid-1960s, most of the Greeks who still lived in Egypt were gone. Only the very poor and old remained, numbering no more than 5,000 from nearly half a million Greeks living in Egypt in the early part of the 20th Century. The era of a long history of Greek presence in Egypt had come to an end. As I write this, more than sixty years have passed from the time we left Egypt. It is a different world today from those days. Many things have changed but the memories of those times are still vivid in my mind.

I have visited Alexandria and Egypt on a few occasions since my departure in 1957, mostly on business trips representing the largest company in the world at the time: Exxon. During these visits, the government of Egypt extended red-carpet hospitalities, recognizing my executive position and their need to do business with Exxon. I have to say even after so many years that passed since we were forced out of Egypt, I enjoyed the attention and respect. It was sort of like a payback. When my official meetings were over, I'd walk alone on the streets in the old neighborhoods with nostalgia and sadness. Everything looked much smaller than what I remembered—the buildings, streets, markets and the tram that I'd taken to school every day. It was a strange feeling, almost like we were never there. All that history, is it forgotten? I struggled with this question for many years until recently.

I was very happy to read an article in the April 26, 2018 issue of the Egyptian newspaper *Ahramonline,* which my friend Peter Chelico shared with me. The publication interviewed Nabila Makram Ebeid, the current Minister of Immigration of Egypt, about acknowledging the large contributions made by the Greeks and other foreigners who once lived in the country. The minister spoke about a new program launched by the Egyptian government "inviting Greeks to return to their roots." The program is called Nostos, a Greek word meaning "a return to roots" or homecoming, particularly to roots near the sea. The program started in Alexandria in May 2018 and was co-hosted by the presidents of Egypt, Greece and Cyprus. In the article, Egyptian President Sassi spoke about their shared Mediterranean history and culture, and the contributions of the Greek communities living in Egypt. The Egyptian government's acknowledgment of this will not return our nationalized properties under President Nasser, but it offers a moral satisfaction that we are remembered.

In the summer of 1957, I was finally on my way to America. I was the first in my family to leave Egypt and I had only $20 in my pocket but was happy to be heading to the United States to study engineering at New York University. I had obtained an exit visa and my ticket to a new life.

My friend Vakis and I boarded a Greek ship in Alexandria to Athens. We arrived at Piraeus port the next day and the ship anchored there for a couple of hours to discharge passengers and refuel. It was a bittersweet bon voyage, as friends came to see us off and wish us well. Tears were choked back and hugs were long and hard as we said our goodbyes, not knowing for certain if we'd ever see each other again. From Piraeus we sailed to Genova and after an emotional separation with my fellow sojourner Vakis, who continued his journey to Switzerland in pursuit of studying hotel management, I boarded the liner Julio Caesar for New York, feeling equal parts scared and excited.

Passage across the Atlantic Ocean seemed like an endless stream of days and nights, daybreaks and sunsets. In some moments, I felt waves of happiness in the crowd of the ship. For the first time in my life, I was among so many Americans returning home from the holidays in Europe. I struck up conversations with a number of them and found them to be a simple, friendly and diverse crowd. For sure they were noisier than the more reserved European crowd I was accustomed to in Egypt.

I made friends easily as the days turned into two solid weeks on the water. Before we arrived stateside, I had gathered a handful of invitations to visit my new friends in their homes. This transatlantic venture was all so thrilling in its uncertainty, yet I was sure of one thing: my desire to start a new life in America, to live in the free land. Like Ulysses in Homer's epic book Odyssey returning to Ithaka, every nautical mile traversed was bringing me closer and closer to my destination—and delivering me to my new safe harbor.

PART TWO
Living the American Dream

4

Coming to America

I would sooner forget my birthday than forget the day I caught sight of Lady Liberty as the SS Julio Ceasar cruised into York Harbor in New York City. It was October 14,1957, and I was nineteen years old. Like most of my fellow passengers, I stood on deck scanning the horizon until the silhouette of the famous statue came into view on Liberty Island. I felt the same warm welcome that she had extended to millions of immigrants who had made passage before me.

My sponsors, Aunt Harriette and her husband, Uncle Louis, greeted me at the dock. They were excited to see me—particularly my aunt, who used to spoil me with English chocolate bars when I was a toddler in Cairo. She loved me then and probably more now that I'd come to live with them. I was like the son she'd never had. I, too, loved my aunt and learned to love my new American uncle.

As we drove through the streets of Manhattan to their home in Astoria, Queens, my senses heightened to take it all in. Along 42nd Street, I watched with quiet awe all of the blinking lights, pedestrians and cars whizzing by. And yet, it wasn't the paradise I'd imagined it to be while back in Egypt. To be honest, it was a letdown for me. In contrast to today, the 42nd Street of 1957 was seedy, run down, dirty and overrun with traffic. It was quite a contrast from what I was accustomed to seeing in Alexandria. The tall buildings made me dizzy and seemed somewhat ominous. I had never seen anything like this city, not even in my dreams.

We finally arrived at Aunt Harriette's house on Ditmars Boulevard, and I remember my first impression. As soon as we walked in the house, Uncle Louis, a TV aficionado, turned on the set. I knew that televisions existed but until that moment, I had never seen one. The first image that appeared on the screen is still forged in my memory: a Savarin coffee commercial with a blonde woman singing, "How good it tastes and how good it is. Drink Savarin coffee!"

SURVIVING UNIVERSITY LIFE

I was finally in America and my new life had begun but those first few years were very challenging for a number of reasons. Once enrolled, I learned that before New York University would admit me into the School of Engineering, I was required to take English language classes at Washington Square College. After four intensive months of immersive language classes, I was officially a mechanical engineering freshman at NYU School of Engineering in the Bronx University Heights campus, located uptown atop a hill. The school was founded in 1854, with its Hall of Fame of Great Americans. (In 1973, NYU sold the campus to the City University of New York because of financial difficulties).

I'd begun to master English but student life was a constant struggle for monetary reasons, as well. Thankfully, I didn't have to pay for housing since I lived with Aunt Harriette. She and my uncle generously provided room and board, and occasionally some limited financial aid towards my tuition. I was grateful for her help but yearned to be on my own and have my own place, no matter how small. I was missing the opportunity to develop friendships and have easy access to resources on campus; plus I wanted the freedom of movement that any young man would want.

In the second semester of my sophomore year, I joined the Delta Phi fraternity on campus. One year later, in my junior year, I was elected treasurer of the fraternity, a position that came with free board at the frat house. Now I had my own room and was living completely on my own . . . a dream come true! My aunt took it hard that I was not going to be living with them anymore. She was a very nice and loving woman but somewhat possessive of me, since they had no children of their own. Yes, they treated me as a son but after a while, I could tell that it was not a healthy situation for me to stay in. It was time to make my own way but I continued to stay close to my aunt for the rest of her life. I made sure that all her needs were met, particularly after her husband Louis passed away in 1975 and until her death in 2007 in Hillsdale, New Jersey. Her kindness and love touched many people and for that we are grateful that she was in our lives.

I worked part time during the winters while taking a full class load, and I worked full time in the summers when classes were not in session. I did whatever it took to earn money. Being a waiter was big money, at least for me. I was a travel agent with Thomas Cook. I worked as a maintenance man at Drake's Bakery in Long Island City. I even served as a counselor in one of the *Herald Tribune's* Fresh Air Funds for inner city kids in Peekskill, New York. They needed somebody to run the trading post at the camp. Somehow I applied for this job and my interview with Ms. Stevens, the director, went better than expected. After the interview, she looked at me and said:

"Okay, young man, I'll give you a chance. You seem to be eager to work."

I remember my heartfelt reply: "This is America and that's why I chose to come here, because in this country you make your own fate, you make your own luck, you make your own life. This is the land of opportunity."
I did not have to say anything more. She understood.

In 1962, I graduated with a bachelor of science degree in mechanical engineering. As I walked across the stage to receive my diploma at the graduation ceremony, I reflected on all the hardships and sacrifices that I had endured to reach that moment. I felt good about who I was and what I had achieved. I'd reached my goal and it was a big milestone in my life, especially being on my own with very little help. After graduation, I quickly secured a New York-based job with Foster Wheeler, one of the largest engineering companies in the States. I was on top of the mountain looking at the world around me with confidence and purpose. The future was bright.

JOINING THE WORKFORCE

During the second semester of my senior year, I had several interviews with engineering companies in different locations and was pleased to receive six job offers. As I just mentioned, I opted to accept a position with Foster-Wheeler, an engineering company specializing in power generation and marine propulsion systems. Their headquarters were located at 666 Fifth Avenue, one of the most prestigious buildings in Manhattan. The deal was that I would join a training program involving travel and assignments outside of New York City for one year with the understanding that at the end of the training period, I would return to the New York office.

During this training, I spent two months in manufacturing facilities in Pennsylvania and upstate New York (Rochester). After that, I was assigned to a nuclear facility in Livermore, California to start up a conventional boiler supplied by my company. While in California, I contacted my mother's cousin, Themis, who lived in San Francisco. Themis was very successful manufacturer of office furniture, obviously wealthy. I liked him although he seemed a bit egocentric. He came to see me at Livermore driving a red convertible Thunderbird and shared that he had a 60-foot sailboat anchored in San Francisco Harbor. Themis was divorced and was quite the lady's man. He had a very nice girlfriend at the time of my visit with him. He invited me to stay in his apartment in San Francisco and gave me the keys to come and go as I pleased, which I did. After that visit, I wanted to stay in contact but somehow the test of time and our busy lives prevented us from doing so. I reached out to him by email at some point but we never saw each other again. A good lesson learned here is to make an effort to stay in touch with relatives, no matter how distant, and with people you like and may need some day.

At the end of my training program, I returned to New York City for a short period of time until the company announced that they were moving to their new headquarters in Livingston, New Jersey. So my dream of having a Fifth Avenue address, unfortunately, did not last long. The commute to Livingston from New York was a non-starter. I spent hours upon hours in the car. On one trip home from work, while listening to the car radio, we heard news that I will never forget: the assassination of President Kennedy. My story is similar to those of other people who remember exactly where they were and what they were doing when that life-altering event happened to our young president and our nation. I liked and admired JFK and his loss was as painful to me as it was for many others in our country.

MEETING DIMITRA

In 1958, I met Dimitra, or Demi, for short. Meeting her was and is the most extraordinary thing that's ever happened to me. We were both students at NYU. I want to go back in time and describe our fateful meeting one night at the international student center in New York City. I vaguely recall the address; it's somewhere in the upper thirties on Third Avenue. Every Saturday night, foreign students would gather, meet old friends and make new ones. We would share experiences, dance, have something to drink (nonalcoholic), sample international hors d'oeuvres prepared by international students, and generally have fun. I was a member of the center and a regular.

One night, my friend Eddie from Egypt and I dropped by after attending another party in the neighborhood. As we were arguing about whether to stay or go back to the party we had just left, I caught sight of this beautiful girl with a long ponytail and dark complexion talking with a young boy across the hall. I was struck by her beauty and her every

Dimitra and me on our first date at Tavern
on the Greene in New York City in 1958.

move, as if I were watching a symphony play in perfect harmony. Little did I know then, that split second would change my life.

"Eddie, I'm staying here," I announced.

He took off for the other party. I waited for a new song to start then walked across the dance hall to where she was standing.

"Would like to you dance?" I asked, a bit nervous but confident.

"Sure," she nodded, nonchalantly.

Being a smart and worldly guy, I began a fascinating conversation with: "I'm Greek. Where are you from?"

She smiled. "Well, guess."

"Okay, Spain."

"No," she said coyly.

"Okay, Portugal."

"No."

"You're from Argentina!"

"Nope."

She had me there on the dancing floor going crazy. I wanted to know where she was from! Finally, feeling sorry for me, she threw me a bone.

"Tell me something in Greek. I know a little Greek."

I've got her now, I thought. *"Se agapo, me agapas."*

"What does that mean? It sounds very nice." Evidently she didn't know these important Greek words.

"It means, 'I love you, do you love me'?"

And then in fluent Greek, she responded: "Well, I don't know if I'm ready to love you yet, but we can work on that!"

I was stunned and also a bit perplexed. "How do you speak so well Greek?"

"Because I'm Greek, stupid!"

That was it, the beginning of tomorrow and the day after and the day after for the next fifty-five-plus years. She had me with that comment and continued to tease me the rest of that evening, I was going around

*Our wedding day on December 28, 1963
in New York City.*

in circles, but this woman clearly had me wrapped around her little finger from that first dance. I courted her for four years but I always turn it around and say that she was the one who chased me for four years. I have come to know her as an incredible soul with a limitless capacity for love. She cares about people and is always sensitive about the needs of others.

We married on December 28, 1963 in the Greek Orthodox Cathedral in New York City. My mother and brother were present, along with my Aunt Harriette, Uncle Louis and some friends. From her side, only uncles and cousins attended since her parents in Greece could not make the trip due to health reasons. We had a lovely reception at our apartment, as it was all we could afford. It was a wonderful feeling to have my partner for life, and to have my mother and brother there to celebrate our union.

Our son, Nicholas, was born three years later at New York University Hospital. He was a beautiful blonde baby with dark eyes. It's funny, both Demi and I are very Mediterranean with dark complexions, and this kid came out blonde. Granted, my father was blonde with green eyes. Dad's sister, Artemis, was also blond with blue eyes. Nicholas (we call him Nick) is the kindest person I have ever known. He has a deep sense of empathy for others and a sharp analytical mind.

Then in 1970, our beautiful girl, Daphne, was born at Englewood Hospital in New Jersey. She was and still is a very special human being, smart, compassionate and beautiful. From the time she was a little girl, Daphne has exhibited the same spirit as her mother: strikingly independent and tenacious, with dark eyes and black hair.

Demi and I enjoyed parenthood but I have to admit that we displayed all the symptoms of inexperienced new parents overprotecting our children when they were growing up in New Jersey; but as you will see later, we didn't allow it to hold us back from giving our children a full and rich experience of the world.

AN ENCOUNTER IN THE DEEP SOUTH

Before I get to that part of the story, I'd like to back up a few years and share something that happened in 1965 before our children were born. After a couple of years working in Livingston, New Jersey, the commute from New York had begun to take its toll. Demi and I were married by then, and I decided to change jobs and relocate to New York. I accepted an offer from M.W. Kellogg, an engineering company specializing in designing and constructing oil refineries and petrochemical plants. One of my assignments was in the field in New Orleans. The company had built an ammonia plant there and was having problems with the steam generation system. A team of engineers was sent to troubleshoot. I was very pleased when I was told that I was selected to be on the team.

So one morning soon thereafter, Demi and I loaded our red Volkswagen Beetle with whatever personal belongings were able to fit in the small trunk and backseat, and began our journey south. We wanted to see more of America, all these places we had read and talked about. We took our time getting to New Orleans, making several stops along the way, including Washington, DC, Williamsburg, the Carolinas, Georgia, Alabama and Mississippi. The South seemed so much different from the North. The trip was not meant to be so peaceful. On the last leg, it was getting late so we decided to overnight at the next exit.

It was summer of 1965 with the Civil Rights Movement at its peak. Freedom Riders, mostly young people, were driving south in their old cars, many in Volkswagen Beetles like ours, to help blacks register to vote. As we drove further into Alabama, feelings of unease and tension filled the air. Every place we stopped, whether to refuel or have a bite to eat, we felt unwelcomed and we weren't sure why.

Finally, we entered the small town of Hayneville, Alabama, the seat of Lowndes County, and pulled into the parking lot of the first motel we came across. We approached the desk to register. The woman took one look at us and then another look through the window at our car parked outside.

"We have no vacancy, buddy, move on," she said sternly.

I tried to explain that we were tired and only wanted to stay for one night. She silently turned around and went into the back room. Within a few seconds, she returned holding a shotgun, and a menacing German

Shepherd accompanied her.

She pointed the gun at us. "Look, we don't like troublemakers here. Move on!"

Demi was petrified and I was very concerned. I calmly showed her my engineering credentials and explained that I was on my way to a work assignment in New Orleans, and that I had nothing to do with the Freedom Riders. I told her that I recognize many "troublemakers" are driving Beetles like the one we were driving but the only reason I was driving a Beetle, I explained, was because we were newlyweds and that's all we could afford.

The woman acquiesced and eventually gave us a room. Then I asked her where we could have a light meal. She gave us directions to the one store in town, a fast food deli, minutes away from the motel. We went back to our car and drove to the deli. We parked and started walking toward the store . . . and then we stopped. There were a few pickup trucks in the parking lot and a half-dozen men leaning against them, with guns in their arms or on the ground near them. The whole scene was surreal, like a scene from the movie Deliverance. Cautiously, we went into the deli. While ordering our sandwiches, I looked outside only to find in horror that a few of the men had begun kicking the tires and shaking our car. I guess they saw my New York plate and didn't like having a Yankee in their parts. They probably assumed that I was "one of those troublemakers."

We were terrified. I suddenly remembered reading in the paper a few days earlier that there was trouble in Hayneville. The article stated that a young priest from Connecticut was shot there during demonstrations. For a few seconds, my whole life flashed before my eyes as I recalled what my father had told me at the farm many years back:

"When a dog chases you, never run away or he will bite you. Stand still and look him in the eyes. The same is true when you confront an angry crowd. If you run, they will kill you."

So instead of panicking, we ordered two hamburgers and French fries to go, and as soon as we saw the crowd pull away from our car, we calmly walked to it, got in and drove away . . . slowly. I kept looking in the rear mirror at the angry men watching us drive away, until they disappeared from sight. Back at the motel, we locked the door and placed a chair against the door handle for additional safety, but we hardly slept that night. At sunrise, we packed our belongings and drove away as fast as we could.

5

My Expanding Career and Family

So there we were, Demi and me, living temporarily in a townhouse complex just outside of New Orleans. In the three short months we resided there, we got our fill of visiting the French Quarter, sampling Creole cuisine and listening to some of the best blues and jazz music in the world; but I was anxious to be reassigned back to the company's New York office. Once back in Manhattan, I stepped into my first supervisory position overseeing a team of six engineers. I welcomed the added responsibility of being in management.

Soon thereafter, I decided to up the ante on myself once more and enroll in a graduate program at NYU. It was a gutsy decision but postponing this would only make it more challenging later when we had children. As it turned out, I completed my master of science degree in Operations Research in 1966, the same year that Nicholas was born—so I guess you could say that our world was expanding in lots of good ways. I cannot say that juggling so many things was easy but we were young and ambitious and determined. I stayed focused on my young family, ensuring that they had a comfortable life. Demi and I decided that she would stay home and care for our children until they were older. So we were busy. Life was good.

In fact, by then, life was made even sweeter by the fact that we now had my immediate family living close to us in New Jersey. In 1962, five years after I had arrived in the States, I was able to bring Takis to New York and help him complete his secondary education at the private Rhodes Preparatory School in Manhattan. He deserves all the credit for being able to not only reenter high school and pick up where he left off in Egypt but going onto be admitted at New York University—and eventually having a successful career in business. I wanted Takis to tell his incredible story in his own words, and he has done so in Part Five.

Shortly after Takis arrived in New York, I arranged for our mother to come live in the States, as well. Finally, we were together in America! A dream had come true. Mom lived with me and after Nicholas was born, she was very happy to babysit her first grandson—who, by the way, is named after his grandfather Nicholas. As I mentioned earlier, four years after Nicholas was born our little Daphne arrived. She was and still is a bundle of joy who made her Yiayia laugh and feel happy (more on Nicholas and Daphne in a later chapter). Together with my brother, we made sure that our mother had everything she needed. It was such a gratifying feeling to see Mom's life become much easier in her later years, and to have her with us until her passing in 1993. In the last few years of her life, mother decided to move to an older adults complex in Hillsdale, New Jersey, near Takis. She had her own one-bedroom apartment and was very happy to be both independent and near her children.

I was posted in Abu Dhabi (more on that later, as well) when I received a dreadful phone call from my secretary in the Abu Dhabi office one day. She had been trying to reach me while I was on a field trip in Sharjah, UAE, to tell me urgent news of my mother. As soon as I got word, I called Takis, who informed me that our mother passed peacefully in the hospital after suffering a stroke.

Demi and I immediately flew to New York for the funeral—one of the longest flights of my life. It was an incredibly emotional day for all of us. We were heartened to see so many people at the funeral, and many were friends that Mom had made in those thirty years she lived in

America. Their presence was a testament to our mother's kindness and affinity to love. A number of her friends got up and spoke. I shared with those who had gathered about her life, including her darkest days in Egypt, and especially her love for her family and her new home, America.

After the church service, everyone followed the casket to the cemetery for the final farewell. In her honor, friends and relatives then gathered after the funeral at a nearby restaurant for the traditional Greek meal called *makaria*. That day, I also shared what Mom was quoted as saying in an interview with the local newspaper just a few months before she died:

Mother and me at our goddaughter Effie's
wedding in Brooklyn in 1983.

*Mother and Nicholas on her 80th birthday
in New Jersey in 1989.*

"I live for today," she expressed from her heart. "I have a good life and am grateful to live here with the freedom I have."

LANDING AT ROCKEFELLER PLAZA

In my work life, I continued to focus my attention on career development outside of engineering, which had its limitations in terms of advancement and earnings potential. My desire was to work for a multinational corporation with global exposure and broad opportunities. After being with M. W. Kellogg for three years, I now felt that I had enough management experience and academic credentials to look for the perfect job.

One day in 1969, I noticed a full-page ad in the Sunday issue of *The New York Times* by Esso International, the international division of Standard Oil Company of New Jersey. (In 1972, Standard Oil changed its corporate name to Exxon Corporation and in 1999, Exxon bought

Mobil Corporation and became Exxon Mobil.) Of course, that was back in the days when companies ran legitimate print advertisements for new hires. I applied and was immediately invited to have lunch at the executive dining room on the top floor of the Esso Building located at Rockefeller Plaza, where the food, service and decor were equal to any five-star restaurant in New York City. At the end of two days of interviews with several managers of various departments, I received a call at home in the evening from the personnel manager. He offered for me to join the company at a salary that was almost twice as much as I had been making in my current job.

Okay, it's a crazy thing to do—and I don't know what gave me the guts to do it—but I politely decline the offer on the basis that the salary was not competitive. I guess I figured that for them to call me at night at my home like that, they must have really wanted me.

I suggested a counter.

"I don't have the authority to change the terms of the offer," the personnel manager responded, "but I will discuss the matter with management and get back to you tomorrow."

Well, I didn't sleep a wink that night nor did I share with Demi my negotiating posture. I didn't want to cause her any anxiety, and I felt confident that I was taking a reasonable risk for a higher reward. The return phone call came early the next morning, sparing me further agony of second guessing my tactic. My counter was accepted and shortly thereafter, I joined the company as an operations engineer in the Aviation Department.

I was so proud of and happy for this achievement. At age thirty-one, it was one of the biggest milestones in my life to date. I would be working with one of the most prestigious companies in America, the largest and most powerful oil company in the States and, by all counts, the top company in the world in terms of revenue. The first day that I walked into my private office on the eleventh floor of the ESSO Building, overlooking the famous ice skating rink at Rockefeller Center, and saw my name placard on the door. I felt empowered and rewarded. It was great feeling of self-confidence and satisfaction. Now I set my sights on proving myself worthy of the challenges ahead. To be sure, all the lessons I learned on the farm back in Egypt about managing people came to bear in my new position, even more than I could have imagined way back then as a young lad. As I will describe shortly, those early experiences not only helped me to survive in what was to be a very competitive work environment and challenging project but also to excel.

Before I continue with my story, I want to take another moment to reflect on that point in my life. When I joined Exxon, I was very proud of how far I had come in the twelve years since my arrival in America from Egypt with nothing more than $20 in my pocket and gratitude for simply being there. A dozen years later, I'd gotten married to Demi, we were blessed with a son (Daphne came later) and I was supporting my young family. I'd earned both a bachelor's and master's degree and helped bring my mother and brother to America. I bought our first house in New Jersey and my mother was close by. To top it all off, I was now working for one of the most prestigious corporations in the world and really enjoying my responsibilities there. I think I'd done well. Hard work and determination were paying off. I was and still am thankful to God for His blessings and presence in my life.

A few short months after I had joined Exxon, my manager called me into his office and asked if I wanted to take over a new project.

"It's a very ambitious project but we feel you have the qualifications to do the job," he said. "You have engineering experience and managerial experience."

"I'm all ears," I replied.

"We want you to help Esso be the first oil company to be ready to fuel the new generation of jumbo jets expected to become operational in one year."

"Tell me more."

"You would be assisting all of our Esso affiliates worldwide by being at all airports where we are delivering fuel for our airline customers."

Esso owned all fueling systems at the airports—from storage tanks, fueling trucks and underground hydrant systems to complete delivery system at all airports, small and large, on every continent. Those systems around the world were not designed to handle the big aircraft that were being manufactured at that time. Esso had to upgrade all of the airports or build new facilities in a coordinated way.

Of course, I said yes to this opportunity, but when I was first put in charge of this project, I couldn't help but wonder: *Here I am, speaking English with an accent, not American born yet I'm expected to go around the world telling people what to do. How do I manage this?* In a way, this challenge mirrored my experience on the farm: a young man overseeing the much older employees. With Esso, as it turned out, every place I visited—whether with Esso employees or working with airport or airline staff—the people were all experienced professionals in their late forties or fifties. I was still in my early thirties.

I decided that the way to work this was to reach out in the Esso global employee pool and personally select a team of the most experienced people I could find from different Esso affiliates around the world. My first choice was an engineer from Esso AG, our German affiliate. The German affiliate was ahead of the rest of the world, designing and testing equipment that could handle the new jets. Then I cherry picked a few representatives from our UK affiliate, and a more senior employee who had worked in the aviation department his entire career. I traversed the globe, filling up the remaining positions with experts from Argentina, Japan and Malaysia. The team had deep experience and was truly international in scope.

Safety of storage and fueling operations, as well as how fast we could fuel the new jets, were our goals. We wrote fueling and safety procedures and developed a design manual, a copy of which was placed on the shelf of every airport where we had a presence. And finally, we completed the design standards for fueling trucks and underground fueling systems at the airports compatible with the new generation jumbo and supersonic commercial aircraft. Whatever our team said, our airport staff, airlines and airport technical employees listened because they knew we had the experience and expertise. We completed our work and met all of our goals in exactly one year from our start date. Not only were we ready but we were also ahead of schedule.

On January 21, 1970, we refueled the first jumbo jet in Frankfurt on Pan American's inaugural flight to New York City. The fueling, a full load of 20,000 gallons, was delivered to the plane using our new equipment within the 45-minute allotted time. This successful operation immediately set high standards for thousands of such fueling operations around the world for years to come. Our mission was accomplished and it was time for me to move onto even greater challenges and opportunities in my career.

TAKING ON THE COMMISSAR

After two years in the Aviation Department, I was transferred to the Economics Department as an analyst in early 1971. This step in my career development prepared me for future managerial jobs. I spent two years there evaluating business opportunities and gaining a valuable understanding of petroleum economics. In 1972, I was happily promoted to the job that I had wanted and lobbied to get for two years: Senior Sales Representative in the International Cargo Sales Department. This department was organized regionally with sales reps responsible for an entire region. I was assigned to South America with primary responsibility selling crude oil from Exxon production that was surplus to our own refinery needs, to third-party customers, mostly government-owned refineries throughout South America.

I realized very quickly that Chile was going to take most of my energies and put me under the spotlight of senior management. Exxon was delivering a large quantity of crude to Chile through a long-term contract at a fixed price, which was signed in the 1960s. Deliveries of supplies to Chile continued uninterrupted for the years while the contract was in effect. In the early 1970s, oil producers like Libya, Saudi Arabia, Venezuela and others unilaterally legislated and levied additional taxes to companies like ours. Standard industry practice was that oil companies would generally recover those taxes from customers and consumers; however, the contract Exxon had with ENAP, the government refinery entity in Chile, did not allow us to pass on additional taxes to the buyer—in this case, ENAP. It was one of those instances where some lawyer added a few words in the contract with significant consequences. Obviously under those conditions, Exxon was stuck with a high-cost supply contract, incurring huge financial losses, while Chile was able to buy crude oil at a cost significantly below the market. We wanted to renegotiate the contract and make it more equitable and also acceptable to Exxon.

Soon after I assumed my new position, senior Exxon management instructed me to open discussions with ENAP and request changes to the terms of the contract. I spent several months traveling back and forth from New York to Santiago, the capital of Chile, negotiating a revision to the contract that was acceptable to both parties: Exxon and ENAP.

Unfortunately, the political climate was not helpful in these negotiations and was always overshadowing them. In 1970, Salvador Allende was elected President of Chile, the first communist to become president of a South American country in open elections. His Marxist policies brought Chile in direct collision with the United States and resulted in severe economic hardships for Chile, including countrywide shortages of everything from food to hard currency. With regards to Exxon's crude oil contract, the Chilean government took the position that we had no legal basis to request revisions.

During my next visit to Santiago, I met with ENAP representatives and tried to bring to the table several commercial proposals but the other side was totally inflexible. Our meetings took place in ENAP's offices in a sparsely furnished conference room—just a long table with six chairs, three on each side. I sat on one side directly facing my opposition: In the center was the commercial director of ENAP; on his right was his deputy, and on his left, a man in his late twenties who was introduced to me as a Commissar of the Communist Party—a committed communist and obviously anti-American.

77

The other two gentlemen were much older than me, in their fifties or sixties with a lot of experience in refineries and commercial operations. Once again, there I was at the negotiating table facing a group of people with diverse experience and political motives. I realized that these discussions were not going to be easy and I had to keep all my options open if I was to succeed in my mission.

This meeting and all subsequent meetings followed the same pattern. We would meet at nine o'clock in the morning. The commissar would open the meeting by standing up and delivering a political speech in Spanish condemning the United States for its policy in South America. He would blurt out many of Fidel Castro's Marxist slogans and after he finished, he would sit down for a few minutes before leaving the room.

After his departure from the meeting, we would spend the next couple of hours discussing commercial alternatives mainly proposed by me, but the discussions did not go too far. ENAP's commercial representatives in the room had instructions from above to hold a hard line at any cost. Every proposal I made was denied.

On my fourth trip to Santiago, I had management approval to make some significant concessions in an effort to resolve this issue. I tested these ideas before I travelled to Santiago with my commercial contacts in ENAP. They felt that the proposed ideas were reasonable but cautioned me that the decision from their side was political. The day of that fourth round of meetings, we met at the usual time and place—only this time, I respectfully requested that the commissar listen to my proposals first before spouting off with his rant. He declined and proceeded to get up and deliver his usual spiel. I was now really annoyed. The moment called for a bold change in tactics—or else, nothing would change.

I had done my homework by reviewing the case with lawyers regarding the prospects of litigation in the courts. I knew how much room I had to maneuver and what was acceptable to us. So now it was time to find another way to break this impasse. I sat quietly, simmering slightly under my collar but calm and collected. As the commissar spoke, I was realistic. I knew that Allende's communist regime was under extreme pressure from the international community and under severe economic duress. The little commissar was a small pawn in a big game, but I had to find a way to get a strong message to the people above who made the decisions. As soon as the commissar finished his speech, I stood up and looked him in the eye with gravity.

"This is the last meeting that I will be attending in Chile," I stated with calm determination. I gave my reasons. "Your speeches, Mr. Commissar, are insulting to me and to my company. This matter is now being put in the hands of our Exxon lawyers and outside counsel to be litigated in international courts."

I got up and left the room.

The ten-minute walk from ENAP's offices to the Hotel Carrera where I was staying seemed to take much longer. I was really nervous about my brazen decision to break up the negotiations and was uncertain that what I was hoping to achieve would come to pass. I psyched myself up by convincing myself that my move was well calculated and I had no better options.

Once back at the hotel, I waited for a visitor from ENAP knocking on my door before noon. It was now 11 o'clock. I was so certain of this that I called room service and ordered an assortment of hors d'oeuvres. I turned on the TV news and waited. About a half-hour later, sure enough, the phone rang. It was reception downstairs, announcing that the deputy director from ENAP was here to see me. I asked them to send him upstairs.

During the next two hours, we polished off all the hors d'oeuvres while drafting a memorandum of understanding (MOU), subject to management approval by both parties, outlining a fair resolution of the contract issues. By the end of the meeting, each of us was eager to review the MOU with our respective managements. I think Pancho (the name of the deputy) and I did well moving this thing forward under extreme pressure and high stakes from both sides.

I left for New York the next day with a firm sense of accomplishment. Finally, I was able to bring our side and their side together. We looked for common ground to find a solution within a commercial framework. It took several discussions after that meeting to complete the negotiations and sign a new contract. A year later, in 1973, Allende was overthrown by force and he killed himself rather than be taken prisoner during a coup by storm troops at his palace.

My takeaways from his experience were invaluable. I learned to 1) listen to my instincts, 2) take calculated risks but make sure I know the limitations of my decisions, 3) never gamble more than what I could afford to lose, 4) have faith in people I trust and 5) that a contract between two parties largely favoring one party will never survive the test of time. With regard to the last point, corporate culture is very important while operating in global markets and resolving conflicts when they occur. Exxon's high standards of ethics and business practices were guiding principles in treating customers and suppliers fairly. My years of experience showed over and over again that our customers and suppliers alike knew that they would be treated fairly in both normal and extreme circumstances.

In the case of ENAP, it became clear that the old contract had become inoperative as a result of fundamental changes in the marketplace due to geopolitical development, where control of crude oil production passed from the private sector to the oil producing countries. Notwithstanding the severe financial losses, Exxon continued to deliver the full contractual volume to ENAP while negotiations were in progress for many months until a mutually acceptable solution was reached. Opting to resolve the conflict through commercial negotiations instead of a harder line, like cutting off supplies and fighting the case in the courts, was the only reasonable approach in the middle of political turmoil and hard times for the people of Chile.

These lessons would continue to serve me well, as I was about to take on my biggest challenge to date in the next few years.

PART THREE
Years in the Middle East

6

Libya and Saudi Arabia

M y competition in Exxon's headquarters was fierce. The professionals working there at my level were handpicked young people with MBA degrees from Harvard and other Ivy League schools. It was Exxon's policy to bring in the brightest and placed them in different jobs and departments in the Rockefeller Plaza headquarters to screen them for top-level positions within the organization. Although my relative competitive position in the group was good up until that point, I felt that I needed a formal MBA to level the playing field and sharpen my communications and analytical skills. So in 1974, I enrolled in a special evening program offered by the New York University Graduate School of Business for young executives who were unable to take time off to pursue a full-time MBA program. In 1976, I completed this program and earned an Advanced Professional Certificate in International Business.

It didn't take long for this academic endeavor to pay off. One early morning in the summer of 1977, I was working and having my coffee at my desk in Rockefeller Plaza when my boss called me into his office. With no introduction, he got directly to the point.

"George, we have another opportunity for you. We are looking to fill a planning manager's position in Esso Libya, our oil producing affiliate there. It is a promotion for you and of course it would be your first managerial position with the company."

"Okay, tell me more," I inquired eagerly. I was up to the task and ready for another new challenge.

"I'll be straight with you, George. Libya is no picnic. Living and working conditions there are going to be difficult but the company will take care of you and your family's needs while you are there." He went onto explain details about the position and what I'd be taking on if I accepted.

"Talk it over with your family," he said at the close of our discussion, "but give us your answer soon."

That evening over dinner, I shared with Demi and the kids the important news. (Daphne was seven years old and was Nick eleven years old at the time.)

"I have an offer to go to Libya on a two-year assignment," I said. "This is a family post and if I accept this offer you will be coming with me."

Their first reaction was one of surprise. It took them a few minutes to realize the magnitude of the news.

"Let's take a vote," I suggested. "We'll make this decision together. If even one of you says no, I'm not going to accept the job."

"What's the political situation in Libya?" Demi wanted to know. I didn't sugarcoat it.

"It's challenging. Gaddafi is running the country and has taken extreme positions with the oil companies threatening nationalization. There will be many challenges for us, but the company will provide good housing, generous travel allowances and opportunities to travel to Europe and Greece."

It didn't take long for us to decide. In spite of the potential pitfalls the whole family voted to seize the experience. I was also very pleasantly surprised about how my mother reacted to this news. While it was difficult for her to have us leave (she was living with Takis by then), she took it well as she saw the opportunities and benefits for us.

"You should go," she encouraged. "I will come and spend time with you when you settle down in your new home."

I promised Mom that as soon as we got situated in Tripoli, I would send for her to come and spend as much time as she wanted. That promise, which was fulfilled soon after we moved into our new home in Libya, made her feel better.

GADDAFI'S GREEN REVOLUTION

At that time, Gaddafi was running Libya in a most bizarre way. He had just launched his "Green Revolution" claiming that the people governed themselves, but in fact he was the dictator. He had nationalized everything. Gone were all private retail stores and only communist-style government cooperatives remained. Shortages of food and other items were common. Getting basic essentials like meat, dairy products and household items was a challenge. We had to go in the black market to secure these basic items and we paid steeply for them. Libya at that time was producing two million barrels of oil a day, commanding a high premium in the European market nearby. This generated billions of dollars of income but the Libyan people saw little benefits from all this wealth. A good chunk of it went to supporting revolutionary movements in neighboring Chad, Kenya, the IRA in Ireland, and elsewhere.

In the meantime and in contrast to what was happening countrywide, we lived a comfortable expatriate life. Exxon provided us with a beautiful villa across the street from the American school and our social lives revolved around it. The school was funded by the American oil companies operating in Libya at the time, which included Exxon, Mobil (they were separate entities then), Occidental Petroleum, Marathon, Amerada Hess and Texaco. The kids had a great experience there and adjusted quickly in their new environment. In fact, they thrived—Daphne as a second grader and Nick as a sixth grader. They had fantastic American teachers, most of them young, enthusiastic and committed.

We lived a typical American suburbia life but on a much smaller scale. Mothers were involved with the PTA and fathers coached basketball and baseball teams. The large school grounds also provided the only outlet for social activities, movies and concerts, exhibitions and book clubs. We lived by the Mediterranean Sea and the climate allowed us to enjoy pristine beaches and clear waters almost year round. But

Daphne and Nicholas with a new acquaintance in the Libyan Desert outside Tripoli in 1978.

most importantly, we had a lot of quality of time together as a family with no TV, no long commutes to work or other big city distractions. Overall, those two years that we lived in Libya, notwithstanding the occasional hardships, were a great learning experience for the kids.

On the business side, I was facing big challenges and getting pressure from the two Libyan members on the board of directors of Esso Libya, who wanted a quick nationalization of my position. The Libyans wanted to put nationals into management and engineering positions, even though the local personnel were not yet ready to assume the responsibilities. Towards the second year of my assignment, our house was taken from us by military officers loyal to Gaddafi. We were given two weeks to move. The company quickly found another villa two blocks away.

Six months later, Gaddafi's People's Committee commandeered our villa and gave it to officials of the "party." It was obvious that they wanted me out to make room for my young deputy, a Libyan engineer and recent graduate of Texas A&M University. Soon thereafter, in the summer of 1979, we were transferred back to Exxon International's headquarters in New York for my next assignment. The physical return to New York from Libya was even more challenging than the move overseas.

When we moved to Libya, Exxon's relocation policy offered their executives to move all their furniture to the new location and at the end of the assignment to return it home at the company's expense. We of course took that option and moved every item in our household back and forth across the ocean. On the return leg and upon arrival in New York, however, the container with our furniture was flooded and most of our belongings had become water damaged. We were compensated by the insurance company for the loss and were able to buy new furniture but we certainly didn't expect to have to part with family items that had grown dear to us for sentimental reasons. Luckily, most of our precious photos were saved. Looking back, yes, they were just material items that could be replaced but at the time, it was an unwelcomed occurrence.

A DIFFERENT DESERT: SAUDI ARABIA

After a year back in New York and happily catching up with family and friends there, I found myself once again waiting to hear details about my next overseas assignment. One morning in the summer of 1980, I met with the senior vice president of Esso Middle East to review specifics of my next posting.

"We're expanding our presence in Saudi Arabia outside the oil sector," he explained. "We've created a new executive position to oversee development of new business opportunities, and it has your name all over it. We'd like you to fill this position. Of course, it comes with a promotion and the usual generous perks that follow expatriates."

I was forty-two years old and by now had a strong preference to stay overseas. I liked the independence and freedom of action that American expatriate executives working for large multinationals like Exxon enjoyed—not to mention the generous financial package and other perks that came along with these jobs. I was uniquely qualified for holding sensitive assignments in the Middle East. I knew the region, I understood its people and local culture, and I spoke Arabic. But I also was fully aware of the risk that the longer I stayed away from headquarters, the higher the chances were of my being forgotten and bypassed for higher executive positions. But I had decided to retire early with maximum benefits and a fast lane for me to achieve that goal was to maximize my overseas service. I discussed my plans with Demi and we both agreed that a good retirement age target was somewhere in my late fifties—old enough to qualify for a pension package and young enough to discover and experiment with new ideas and experiences. I wanted to try something different in another industry, while enjoying more time with my family in a stress-free environment with no financial concerns.

So I pushed the discussion with the senior VP along these lines and even though I knew the answer, I asked, "What happens after I complete this assignment? I would like be considered for other overseas positions as they open up."

"We cannot foresee what openings will be available in two years but we will keep your interests in mind," he replied.

Exxon's presence in the Kingdom of Saudi Arabia dates back to 1944 when Standard Oil Company of New Jersey (Esso) and Socony-Vacuum Oil Company (Mobil) became part of ARAMCO. Oil production at that time was 20,000 barrels per day. By 1980, production had reached ten million barrels per day. In the same year, the Saudi government completed the gradual buyout of ARAMCO's assets from the American oil company partners.

As usual, this offer to move to a new country was discussed with my family. This time we were somewhat skeptical to accept the offer to go to Saudi Arabia for two years. Life for expats in the kingdom was restricted. The good news was that the International School in Riyadh had impeccable credentials. Schooling for our children was one of the most important criteria in evaluating an offer to assume a posting overseas. The kids were again excited about the prospect of moving back overseas. By this time, Daphne was nine years old and Nick was thirteen.

"Ah, sure, lets go! Why not?" they responded. "We'll meet some new friends. We'll travel."

Demi had a more tepid response: "Ah, okay, I don't really want to go, but you know what? Let's try it for two years and make the most of it."

In the 1980s, Saudi Arabia was booming. The newly acquired wealth from oil revenues had a big impact on the kingdom. Modern buildings were rising everywhere. A new airport was under construction in Riyadh. Superhighways were laid out across the desert like giant snakes, crawling through the sand dunes. Supermarkets and fancy restaurants were opening everywhere. Shopping malls were full of local women window shopping and buying expensive designer clothes and gadgets, dressed in their "Abayas", the black national dress, which covered them from head to toe. They were required to dress conservatively when outside and women were not allowed to drive.

On busy city streets, Mercedes and BMWs and Toyotas were stuck in traffic with only male drivers behind the wheels. High-end restaurants with gourmet menus, plush decor and crystal glassware on the tables served sumptuous meals with glasses of orange juice or soda. Alcohol was strictly prohibited throughout the kingdom. I've always felt that a good meal is wasted when not accompanied by a glass of fine wine, so we seldom ate out.

We decided to live in the city, a short drive from the office. The company provided us with a beautifully furnished villa. We were allowed to buy all of the furniture in the US and have it shipped to Riyadh. The kids had to be driven to school and Demi had to be driven everywhere. We had a designated driver from the Philippines named Silver and the kids liked him. He was kind to them and drove them around to school, baseball and swimming practices, and shopping with Demi. The loss of freedom of movement, however, is something that we take for granted in our western society, and it was difficult for Demi to accept.

In our spare time, we took every opportunity available to do things, explore and learn. We went on trips into the desert; in one locale, we unearthed and collected petrified fossils and seashells. Most of that region was underwater when dinosaurs roamed the Earth. During school breaks, we travelled outside the kingdom. We spent one Christmas in Singapore, holidays in Malaysia and Hong Kong, and summers back home in New York and New Jersey.

KING ABDUL AZIZ'S PALACE

One day, we joined friends and their children—two boys and three girls (the boys were the same age as Nick and the girls a little older than Daphne—and embarked on a search for King Abdul Aziz's old palace. King Abdul Aziz was born around 1880 and had many wives and numerous children. He was the founder of the Kingdom of Saudi Arabia, which is named after him still today. His sons succeeded him to the throne and the present King Salman is the last of his surviving sons occupying the throne. We had read much about Abdul Aziz's original palace, probably built in the early 1900s, located south of Riyadh, but we did not have the exact location. After a couple hours of driving around (no GPS in those days), we arrived at this broken gate with a guard sitting on a bench, half asleep. I asked him in Arabic if he would give us directions to the palace.

"Here!" he said, waving his arm behind him.

We asked if we could drive in and he nodded. We drove down a dirt road until we arrived at the old palace, which was showing signs of neglect and weathering of time. It was empty. The kids got out of the car, excited and ready to explore.

Before we could stop them, they entered the palace and disappeared.

I got worried about them being alone and I followed them to the second floor of the structure. I left the rest of the group down below in the yard, who were talking, drinking some water and relaxing after the long drive. Then I heard screams.

"George! Come, come!"

I looked down and saw two parked Toyota SUVs with four Saudis dressed in their national white dress and traditional head dress, the "Ghutrah", screaming at my group in Arabic. I raced down to see what was going on.

"Hey, what's going on here?" I asked in Arabic to the man who seemed to be in charge.

"Well, you're not supposed to be here. This place is off limits. All of you come with me. I am taking you to jail!"

"What is your name, sir?" I asked. He told me his name was Abdullah.

"Wait a minute," I responded. "I'm sorry, I asked the guard at the gate and he said we could go in."

"How come you speak Arabic?" he prodded.

"Well, you know, I live here. I like the people and I made it a point to learn your language."

He reflected for a minute. "All right, your people can stay here. You come to jail with me."

I obeyed and continued to speak to him in Arabic.

"Abdullah, let me ask you a question. Suppose you and your family and friends, who don't speak English, traveled to my city, New York, and went to visit the tallest building in Manhattan, the Empire State Building. You ask permission and they tell you that you can enter the building. You go in and when you are on the top floor, enjoying the Manhattan skyline, they come in and say, 'No! You're not supposed to be here!' And they take you to jail, leaving your children and women behind in a strange place. How would you feel about that?"

I knew that as soon as I mentioned women, I'd hit a sensitive cord. Local culture and customs regard women's honor and safety as the high-

91

est priority. Abdullah hesitated for a minute and then replied.

"You know, you're right. That's not fair. Give me the film from your camera and you are free to leave."

My friend, Chuck, who was standing behind me, handed over his camera and whispered in my ear:

"No way I will give up the film! I have all my Christmas pictures on it."

Inconspicuously, he instead handed me a blank film, which I gave to Abdullah. He put it in his pocket and after a few customary salutations he gave us the okay to leave.

"Stop by my office the next time you're in Riyadh and let's have tea together," I said to Abdullah.

At that moment, Demi had to interject:

"George, ask him where is the nearest souk [market]." Demi is an avid collector of Bedouin jewelry, and a frequent visitor to every souk in Riyadh. She knew almost every Bedouin jewelry vendor there. Abdullah explained how to get to the souk, but it got too complicated so he volunteered to take us there.

We got in our cars and followed him. He drove out of the palace onto the main road, jumped the divider and began heading in the opposite direction. We didn't want to lose him, so we followed his lead. It was clear that he was the man in charge now. Breathless, we finally arrived to our destination, parked the car and disembarked.

Abdullah approached our car. "We have to walk a little bit," he explained.

We began walking towards the square of the small town with me and Abdullah in front and the rest of the group in the rear. As we're walking, he reached down to take my hand. Now we are walking holding hands. In Saudi Arabia and in the Arab world, two men holding hands is an expression of friendship. It has no other connotation. I felt very good about it because here is a guy I met only one hour ago under adverse conditions, and now he is my friend.

We finally reached the main square, with my friends and our children following behind us and pedestrians and shopkeepers watching us as we proceeded to find the store selling Bedouin jewelry. For onlook-ers, this must have been some sight: a Saudi man in his national dress walking in the middle of the square, holding hands with an American in jeans, a T-shirt and baseball cap. Then suddenly I felt Nickolas push me slightly with his shoulder.

"Dad," he whispered in my ear.

"What is it, Nicholas?"

"Put your hands in your pockets, Dad. Some of my friends are here and they're watching. Please put your hands in your pockets."

And then I realized how embarrassed my teen-age son must had been seeing his father holding hands with this guy in front of all his friends. Later I explained to him what it meant but he wasn't inclined to forgive me for the embarrassment I had just caused him.

BOOTLEGGING IN THE BATHROOM

In Saudi Arabia, alcohol consumption is strictly prohibited on religious grounds. The penalty for breaking this law is deportation for expats, and flogging and jail for Muslims. The truth is that most of the expats had access to alcoholic beverages and many Saudis, particularly military personnel, consumed alcoholic beverages. With the right connections and some money, anything could be bought on the black market. The price for a bottle of Black Label scotch whiskey was as high as $200, depending on the demand. In times of shortages, prices skyrocketed. On one of those occasions, my neighbor and landlord, Saleh, a major in the Saudi Air Force, told me an interesting story.

One day, American-supplied military AWAC airplanes patrolling the northern border picked up activity showing a convoy of trucks cross-ing the border. Fighter airplanes were scrambled, and National Guard units were dispatched to the boarder to stop what they thought was an invasion of unfriendly forces. To their surprise, what they found was bootleggers moving a fully loaded convoy of trucks with contraband alcoholic beverages.

Some people also made their own booze. It was easy to get our hands on an underground "manual" compiled by ARAMCO expats showing how to build small, homemade stills and how to distill and make pure drinking alcohol from those stills. The still I had was really simple. It consisted of a pressure cooker, a thermometer at the top of the cooker, and a copper coil running from the top of the cooker to a bucket below, filled with water, acting as the condenser. Wine was easy to make. All we had to do was to buy bottles of Rauch, a German brand of grape juice with no additives, add yeast, wait twenty-one days, and voila we had homemade wine. The truth is, the white wine was surprising good, but we were never able to make drinkable red wine.

For obvious reasons, I wanted to keep this winemaking activity under control and not visible to guests and workers visiting the house. So I kept all the equipment in my private spacious bathroom by the bedroom. Of course, the wine fermentation made percolating noises, something that Demi never got used to as she was showering in the morning. Despite her constant requests to move the equipment to another room in the house, I was determined to keep this clandestine operation safe and hidden from intruders, and the odds of someone coming into our master bathroom were next to never. At times, Saleh, our landlord, would send me a few bottles of real wine or scotch. We were always fully supplied with whatever we needed to give some great parties, where we shared experiences and a laugh or two with friends and business associates about our experiences in the kingdom.

After two years in the kingdom, Nicholas had graduated from junior high school in Riyadh and unfortunately there was no American high school available in Saudi Arabia. Our options were to send him to boarding school in Europe or the United States, or request that the company reassign me back to New York. Nicholas did not want to go to boarding school so we requested reassignment. Exxon was always very understanding when family issues came up with expatriate executives serving overseas. They worked on my request and promptly found an executive opening for me in the New Jersey headquarters. Within a couple of months, we had returned once more to our old neighborhood in Old Tappan near family and friends.

7

Abu Dhabi and Kuwait

At the risk of giving the impression that life was one big jet-setting adventure in exotic countries, I'd like to give equal weight to the many challenges that kept presenting themselves in my life. I am grateful to God for all the goodness and experiences, even the ones that were painful or daunting.

While in Saudi Arabia, one year before we returned home, Demi noticed a small lump on my neck. The local doctors were not able to diagnose its origin and we were concerned that it might be something serious. During one of my visits to New York, I consulted with several physicians and finally went to see a head-and-neck specialist at Brookhaven Hospital. He was also concerned that the growth might be cancerous and recommended that I have immediate surgery, which we did.

In the OR, the surgeon discovered that the growth was a very rare benign carotid body tumor near my brain. As the team of doctors made preparations to remove the tumor from the artery, my friend, Dr. Adel Abadir, who was present in the OR at my request, stopped the lead surgeon midstream. He recommended right then and there that the tumor be removed by a vascular surgeon, as the procedure was very delicate and risky in nature due to the tumor's proximity to neural pathways in the brain. Since it was a benign tumor, he later stated, it was okay to wait to have the second surgery.

So as soon as we returned to New York from Saudi Arabia, I scheduled the operation with renowned vascular surgeon Dr. Joe Imparrato. I was in the operating room for many hours and the doc reported afterwards that the procedure was tricky but I was in good hands. In the end, I recovered quickly and all is well. This situation brought home to me the preciousness of life and how important it is to live it fully.

As far as work was concerned, after a long recovery, I was back at Rockefeller Plaza in the position of commercial manager with Exxon International. The team that I was in charge of was responsible for buying supplies of crude oil for Exxon's worldwide refineries. We negotiated large supply contracts with both private organizations and government agencies. My geographic area of responsibility remained the Middle East due to the knowledge and expertise I had accumulated over my years there.

On the family and home front, we decided to sell the house we had been renting while we were overseas and move near Takis and his wife, Paula, who also resided in Old Tappan, New Jersey. Mom was living with them by then so this made a lot of sense. Takis had an Olympic-sized swimming pool and the kids loved to swim with their friends. We had great parties and made beautiful memories. Nicholas and Daphne acclimated well into the local public high school. Nicholas quickly became active in athletics and made the basketball varsity team. Daphne took up all kinds of activities related to music, sports and academics.

I continued to travel a lot for my job, visiting the Middle East several times a year to meet with suppliers and government officials. I always looked forward to coming back home to enjoy my family and suburban life in New Jersey—which we did for five years after my repatriation from Saudi Arabia.

But then Exxon began to experience difficult times. It was 1985 and the oil industry was going through adjustments after the rapidly rising of cost of buying oil from producers who had become aggressive and independent. Overproduction and decreased demand drove oil prices down, putting pressure on revenues and profits. In response to market conditions and after years of growth, the company had become top heavy—too many managers and executives drawing large salaries. In response, Exxon was the first oil company in the industry to downsize. They closed offices, offered incentives for early retirements and began to place more people out in the field. In a short period of time, Exxon International moved their headquarters from New York to New Jersey and reduced staff.

Of course, this had a trickle-down effect for me. My position was eliminated and I was asked to take a new senior position in Abu Dhabi, representing Exxon in the Middle East in commercial and supply operations. It was a new position tailored to my area of knowhow and experience. Although at the time Demi was not very happy to relocate again, in retrospect, it was the perfect job for me. As it turned out, it was a very enjoyable and rewarding experience for her, as well.

So there we were once more, making plans to move back overseas; this time, it would be just Demi and me. By then, Nicholas was already in his first year at Colgate University in Hamilton, upstate New York. Daphne's situation was more complicated. There was no suitable high school in Abu Dhabi, only an English curriculum school, but she felt that this was not a good choice for her. Demi and Daphne decided that boarding school was the best option. I was not in favor of the separation but this is what they both wanted. Daphne applied at Exeter, a prestigious prep school in New Hampshire, and was accepted. Within a couple of months, both of the kids were settled at their schools and Demi and I had moved to Abu Dhabi.

Life was good there in the sense that the country was in the middle of an economic boom and everything was available. The ruler of the United Arab Emirates (a country that consists of Abu Dhabi, Dubai, Sharjah, Fujairah, Ras Al Kheima and Khor Fakkan) was Sheikh Zayyed Al Nahayan. He was very progressive and took care of his people. He launched an ambitious five-year program using the vast income from oil to build new facilities, houses and hospitals. The whole city was humming with economic activity and construction.

My job was highly challenging yet rewarding. I traveled throughout the region interacting with high government officials and private businessmen. By then I had become an important Exxon player in the Middle East. As a senior representative, Demi and I had an active social life interacting with the business and diplomatic community—which we enjoyed to the fullest. We attended some great parties and often hosted fun parties ourselves. During our dozen years living there, we hosted many visitors from abroad, including relatives and friends; during those visits, we traveled the region to interesting sites and learned about the cultures of the people of the Arabian Peninsula.

A Greek party at home with Demi and our friend, John, improvising a Syrtaki Greek dance.

On my boat with Takis in Abu Dhabi in 1993.

REELING IN SAILFISH

One of the many perks of my job in Abu Dhabi was that I had much less of a commute to work, a more flexible schedule and more free time to enjoy things we liked to do. We lived by the sea, with a panoramic view of the Arabian Gulf and first-class facilities to enjoy water sports. I had two boats: a 300-horsepower outboard Boston Whaler, one of the best recreational boats ever built, and a Sunfish sail boat. Demi and I loved to fish in the Persian Gulf—one of the best fishing spots in the world—and the Boston Whaler was the perfect boat for that. With my Sunfish, I sailed solo on the coastal waters around the island of Abu Dhabi. The weather in the summer gets very hot and humid, with temperatures as high as 120 degrees Fahrenheit, but the winters are mild and pleasant. So we always took summer vacations to escape the heat and spent the rest of the year in this nearly perfect climate.

The kids came to Abu Dhabi for Christmas and Easter and they enjoyed their visits immensely. Nicholas loved to scuba dive in the Persian Gulf and in Fujairah in the Indian Ocean. Daphne, the social ambassador of the family, would make friends and spend time doing what college kids do while on a school break. She especially liked to sand ski. It's quite an experience using a snowboard to ski down the mountainous dunes in the desert!

Our favorite activity during the kid's visits was to take our Boston

Me and my friend, John, catch a sailfish after 35 minutes of reeling it in (Abu Dhabi in 1990).

Whaler out to a small nearby island and camp and swim. The island had a small cove with dolphins nearby. We would often see pods of dolphins swimming in and out of the cove. As soon as we'd enter the cove, Daphne would jump in the water and soon small pots of dolphins would begin swimming around her like they were welcoming her into their world. Soon Daphne and the dolphins would form a group of playmates, enjoying each other's presence. After several visits, I could not help but believe that the dolphins expected Daphne's visits and were happy every time she returned to join them for a swim in their turf.

And of course what we enjoyed quite a bit was fishing. Nicholas and I would take the boat out into the Persian Gulf. It's a rich fishing ground with many species of fish, including porgies, groupers, mackerels, cobias and enormous sailfish. Fishing for sailfish required skill and patience, as they are enormous fish weighing more than ninety pounds. When hooked, they fly high out of the water and into the sky before splashing back down, thus the name sailfish. I started a catch-and-release practice with other fishermen. Any sailfish we caught were released unharmed after being tagged so we could track them and study their habits and migration patterns. We learned that sailfish can travel long distances.

GOLFING ON THE BROWNS

Demi and I joined the Emirates Golf Club in Dubai and became avid golfers. While Abu Dhabi was constructing a multi-million dollar championship golf course, we also played on its old so-called "desert course"—a flat piece of dry land with no vegetation. For greens, we used fine sand mixed with oil to keep the sand from blowing away. We called them "browns." To eliminate footprints and ball marks from the greens, attendants would stand by with brooms, sweeping and smoothing out markings left after the players were done putting. The fairways were marked with stakes. We played on that course for a couple of years until finally a championship course was completed in Abu Dhabi.

Golfing at the Emirates Golf Club in Dubai
with Demi and Takis in 1993.

During the time that we played on the desert course, we participated in regular tournaments and won a few trophies, particularly Demi. She was a more competitive player. We succeeded in having our names posted on its club wall, celebrating a rare achievement for a golfer. We both had a hole-in-one on the same hole—the ninth, par 145 feet—one year apart to the day. Golfers who read these lines will appreciate how rare this is—especially both of us getting the same hole-in-one on the same hole!

RIDING THE DUNES

Another extraordinary experience that we enjoyed while in the Emirates was our trips to the Empty Quarter and its mountainous dunes. These dunes were very high, sometimes reaching 100 feet. They were made of fine sand with a perfect blue sky above them. All you could see as far as the eye could stretch was the vastness of the land. Days were sweltering but the nights were cold and spectacular. The sky was

Demi in the Arabian desert in 1989.

always filled with millions of stars and quietness; only the whisper of the wind could be heard across the Empty Quarter.

Driving in the desert and riding the dunes were experiences that required knowing what you were doing. We learned how to navigate the large Toyota SUVs across the sand; if not done properly, the vehicle

Driving across the dunes.

would sink, making it difficult to dig it out without a lot of cursing.

Another activity that we enjoyed was visiting and exploring neighboring countries. Oman was my favorite country, located at the bottom of the Arabian Peninsula. Its unique beauty offers spectacular coastlines stretching from the Strait of Hormuz in the Persian Gulf along the Gulf of Oman and the Arabian Sea to the border of Yemen. The combination of green mountains and desert of reddish-yellow sand adds a special aura to the impressive landscape.

The kids loved our visits to Oman and enjoyed staying at its landmark hotel: The Bustan Palace in Muscat, the capital. This hotel was inaugurated in 1985 by Sultan Qaboos, the ruler of the Sultanate of Oman. He commissioned the Cypriot construction company Joannou & Paraskevaidis (J&P) to build the hotel with the proviso that it be ready to open in the summer of 1985 to host the Gulf Cooperation Council (GCC) summit in Muscat the same year. I was told by local government officials that the owner of J&P, G. Paraskevaidis, personally met with the Sultan to assure him that the hotel would be ready for the conference. During construction, multiple crews worked around the clock

At night, the construction site was flooded with lights, as hundreds of workers and engineers worked to meet the deadline. The keys to the hotel were delivered personally to the Sultan by Paraskevaidis in time for the summit. I was told by local sources that the construction cost for the 240-room resort was $240 million, or $1 million per room. Every time we stayed there, whether during a business trip or when visiting with the

Dad hard at work, getting unstuck in the dunes.

family, we often jokingly reminded ourselves that we were sleeping on a $1 million bed.

I have traveled throughout Oman in the mountains and along the coast, and the land always fascinated me with its majestic beauty and history. There is so much one can write about Oman but this is not the place; however, I will share on these pages a few thoughts and photographs about the spectacular Musandam Peninsula overlooking the Straits of Hormuz, guarding the gateway to the Arabian Gulf and the northern entrance to the Indian Ocean.

The peninsula is sparsely populated by the Shihuh, a semi-nomadic people who live in their ancestral mountain homes in the winter season when the temperate climate allows an outdoor life. In the summer, they migrate to the valley to find work in coastal settlements. This region of Oman has been known to Greek and Roman geographers and is famous among fishermen and seafarers for its rugged land of high mountains, deep valleys and fjords, similar to ones I had seen along Norway's coast years earlier. To describe it adequately, it may be appropriate to quote the Norwegian explorer Thor Heyerdahl who penned his impressions upon approaching Musandam from the upper gulf on his boat, the Tigris:

"The sky was blue above us, but there was a white cloud - banks along the entire horizon ahead. Cloud-banks, but what the devil did we see above the clouds? I grabbed the binoculars . . . for a moment I can hardly believe my eyes. Above the cloud-banks, raised above the earth was land, like another indistinct world of its own. Solid rock was sailing up there, still so far away that the lower parts seemed transparent and did not even reach down into the cloud; the upper ridge seen against the clear sky was of different shade of blue . . . Were we heading for the Himalayas? Was it an optical distortion, a *Fata Morgana?* The whole peninsula was a lofty mountain chain with rock walls dropping almost perpendicular into the sea . . ."
—Excerpted from *Musandam* by Paolo Costa, Immel Publishing (London 1991)

A CLOSE ESCAPE BEFORE THE INFERNO

On July 30, 1990, Demi and I boarded a British airways flight at JFK Airport for London. We had just spent a month vacationing in the United States with family and were heading back home to Abu Dhabi. Demi disembarked in London to visit some friends and I connected with another British Airways flight to Bagdad. My plan was to stop in Bagdad for a short visit to finalize ongoing negotiations with the Iraqis concerning the purchase of liquefied natural gas from the Iraqi government.

After Iraq, I wanted to also stop in Kuwait to push forward stalled negotiations for a large contract of crude oil. I was looking forward to finishing these discussions quickly then finally going home to Abu Dhabi. I arrived at the airport in Bagdad early on the morning July 31 and was met by government officials to clear me through customs and passport control. The developments in Iraq and threats by Saddam Hussein towards his neighbors, and particularly Kuwait, had me worried.

I went directly to the office of the Iraqi Oil Ministry where I met with the deputy marketing director with whom I had a solid long-term relationship. His wife was English and he always had a good story to tell. After the customary welcoming small talk, I tried to gear the discussion towards the purpose of my visit and press for a conclusion of the contract; but progress was slow and it seemed that the issues on the table were minor. I was fully aware that the political current environment was tense, with Saddam Hussein threatening military intervention in Kuwait unless the Emir of Kuwait met his demands for settling border issues, OPEC crude oil production levels and payments of money Iraq owed the Kuwaitis, which they could not meet.

I was familiar and comfortable with the nonlinear style of negotiations in that part of the world where progress is slow and indirect; however, these discussions were different. I sensed that they really did not want to talk. One hour into the meeting and after several cups of tea, the deputy looked me in the eyes and suggested that this was not a good time to have these discussions. I immediately got the message so I told him that I fully understood and would be happy to return at a later date after things settled down.

My friend made a car available to me with a driver for the duration of my visit. He suggested that I might wish to visit the newly renovated ancient city of Babylon, which had just reopened for visitors. I thanked him for the offer but said I'd been away from my Abu Dhabi office for a long time and needed to get back to take care of many pending issues waiting on my desk.

A few hours later, I boarded the first flight out of Bagdad for Kuwait. Upon arrival at Kuwait International Airport, I was met by a small delegation of friends from the Kuwait Petroleum Company (KPC). The atmosphere at the airport was tense, with soldiers and police everywhere. Even with the assistance of KPC people, it took us longer than usual to clear customs and security. After we cleared the airport, I went directly to the hotel where I found a message from a senior KPC person advising that they had arranged a luncheon meeting the following day. It was to be held at the revolving restaurant atop the Kuwait Towers Building, a prestigious landmark in Kuwait City.

The next day, I was picked up at the hotel a little before noon and taken to the restaurant. The lunch was pleasant, with several KPC people in attendance. It was immediately obvious that this group had no intention of discussing business. They were more interested and eager to hear news from my visit to Baghdad. I told them that I'd found people in Baghdad tense for the same reasons that they were tense in Kuwait. I didn't know anything more than what the newspapers and TV media had been reporting, the same news they had heard from watching CNN and the BBC.

At the end of the lunch, I asked them to make arrangements for me to catch the first flight out of Kuwait for Abu Dhabi. I boarded my flight at eight o'clock local time and two hours later landed in Abu Dhabi. Omar, our driver, was waiting outside the customs area and I was happy to see his smiling face. By the time I arrived home in Abu Dhabi, it was close to midnight on August 1. I was happy to be home safe and sleeping in my own bed. It was too late to call Demi to tell her that I was home safe; she was still in London waiting for clearance to fly to Abu Dhabi. At four o'clock in the morning on August 2, my phone rang and startled me out of my sleep. It was Demi calling from London. I could tell right away that she was very worried. She asked if I was home safe.

"Of course I am home," I said. "You just called our house number and woke me up! What's up?"

I was half asleep but made out what she was saying: Saddam Hussein's army had crossed the Kuwait border in a full-scale attack and had taken Kuwait City. I hung up and turned on the TV. It was all over the news. I was one of the last people to leave Kuwait before the Iraqi army moved in. The first thing the Iraqis did after they crossed the border was

*Smoke above Abu Halifah in southern
Kuwait in 1990.*

to bomb the airport and shut it down. The last flight that landed in Kuwait was a British Airway's flight from Australia, which arrived shortly after my departure. The passengers of that flight were not allowed to leave and were taken hostage by Iraq.

It took several months and intense negotiations before these passengers were released. I was a very lucky man to cut my Iraqi and Kuwait visits short and listen to my instincts and return to Abu Dhabi earlier. If I had kept my original schedule I would've been taken hostage, a guest of Saddam's in an Iraqi prison, waiting for my release. The occupation of

Kuwait lasted seven months and led to the first Gulf War.

President's Bush successful efforts to bring together a coalition of forces of European and Arab nations under the command of General Norman Schwarzkopf crushed the Iraq occupational forces and liberated Kuwait. During the occupation, Iraqi civilian and military forces used brutal force to destroy military and non-military installations in Kuwait. Six hundred oil-producing wells in the desert where set ablaze. The refinery outside Kuwait City was totally destroyed. Government buildings and commercial enterprises were sacked. Computers, fine art, automobiles, even luxurious yachts belonging to the royal family and wealthy

Oil wells on fire in Kuwait.

Kuwaitis were stolen and taken to Baghdad or other locations in Iraq or elsewhere. The pipeline feeding crude oil to the refinery in Kuwait City was cut and rerouted to the sea, pumping oil into the Persian Gulf for seven months and causing huge environmental problems.

Many young Kuwaitis were killed and many more were taken prisoner. By the time Kuwait was liberated, the country was in ruins. I stayed in Abu Dhabi for two months from the beginning of the hostilities to make sure that all dependents were out of the country. After that period, there was nothing more to do in Abu Dhabi and I decided to move to headquarters in New Jersey and conduct my business from there for about five months until the war was over. On February 29, 1991, after Kuwait was liberated and Iraqi forces retreated back to Iraq, I returned to Abu Dhabi to pick up where we had left off seven months earlier. After my return, my first order of priority was to visit Kuwait as soon as possible, but management in New York felt that it was not safe for me to do that just yet.

In the end, I persuaded management to give me the clearance and shortly after liberation I was on a plane to Kuwait. I was aware from intelligence reports of the destruction to the infrastructure caused by Iraqi occupational forces. My flight from Abu Dhabi to Kuwait was empty with the exception of the crew and a couple of security personnel. The two-hour flight from Abu Dhabi to Kuwait was uneventful until we reached Kuwait airspace. Cruising at 36,000-feet altitude and looking out the window, everything looked normal. As we approached the airport and the plane began its descent, the sky began to change. First, the sun disappeared as we reached lower altitude. We were now inside a thick black cloud. When we reached 10,000-feet altitude, the black cloud began to get thinner and suddenly I saw the ground. My first reaction was disbelief. For a brief moment, I thought I was seeing a live version of Dante's Inferno where he describes his plunge into the very depths of hell. The desert below was blazing. Six hundred oil wells were on fire and plumes of black smoke were rising everywhere, blackening the sun and everything else. It was a sight I will never forget.

We landed safely at the airport where security was extremely tight. I made it through the first checkpoint and saw my KPC friends waiting for me outside the security zone. After elaborate questioning by security officers, I joined my friends in the empty airport. We embraced and exchanged emotional nods and few words. It was clear that this moment was poignant for both them and me.

As I recovered from this shock, I looked at the white national dresses my friends were wearing and something appeared strange to me. I carefully looked again and asked what had happened to their dresses, as they were covered with oil stains from top to bottom.

"How did you get so dirty?" I asked, a little perplexed.

They explained that the air was so polluted from the oil droplets and smoke raining down that standing outdoors even for a few minutes was time enough to soak their clothing.

As we drove back to the city, the destruction was evident everywhere. It took several months to douse the fires and years to reconstruct the country.

8

Customs and Culture

M y time in the Middle East was, of course, not all about business. As I have alluded to already, it was largely about experiencing the world and becoming intimately familiar with other cultures,
other peoples, other ways of living. To that end, I would like to share a
few more stories.

FIRST-CLASS FALCONS

On one of my trips to Doha in Qatar, I finished my business early and
rushed to the airport to fly home to Abu Dhabi. I was typically late getting to the airport due to my work schedule, and I was usually the last
one on the plane. This day was no different. I boarded the aircraft and
found my seat in first class. As I got settled in, I noticed some strange
companions in the cabin.

First class had many seats but only two people: myself sitting in a
window seat and in the front row was a Sheikh, a member of the royal
family. All of the other passenger seats were occupied by falcons. Yes,
birds! They all had tiny hoods on their heads covering their eyes. Be-

lieve me, it was quite a spectacle. Each falcon occupied its own seat, perched on a board placed on top of the seat. There were no cages. The only thing securing them was a light chain attached to one leg and the other attached to the seat. I sat down, a little incredulous, while the winged passenger next to me just perched there, quiet, sensing my presence next to it as if I were the odd one on the flight. This is too much, I thought. Birds of flight on a flight! An aviary of aviation.

Naturally, I was concerned about how these birds would react upon takeoff and landing but the flight crew didn't seem to be the least bit worried. As the plane began to taxi on the runway, I buckled up and braced myself for any unfriendly movements from my winged companion next to me. The bird shook its wings, perhaps sensing the roar of the engines underneath, but stayed calm, almost motionless, during liftoff.

As soon as the "fasten your seat belt" sign was turned off, I stood up and glanced back at the economy class section. Half of it was filled with falcons, all ensconced peacefully on their seats. Just then, a man walked into the first class section from the rear and carefully inspected each bird.

"What is your name?" I asked when he approached my seat.

"Mohammed," he responded.

"Are you in charge of all these birds?"

"I'm their keeper and trainer, yes." He went on to say that the falcons belonged to Sheikh Al Thanni, a cousin of the ruler of Qatar, pointing to the man in the front row.

"Why are all these falcons on the plane?"

"Well, the Sheikh every year takes his birds to Pakistan to hunt."

"Interesting. Tell me more." He was happy to accommodate my request.

"The Bedouins used falcons in the old days," he went on to inform me. "They would hunt rabbits and small gazelles in the desert. This tradition has been kept alive and today wealthy people use the falcons to hunt as a hobby. However, nothing is left in the desert to hunt anymore. So the sheikhs and rich people take their falcons and their entourage to Pakistan to hunt."

He continued to enlighten me about how they rent an entire area exclusively for their use for a period of time, maybe two weeks or a month. I was told that the rental fee for the use of the land sometimes is as high as $1 million a day, a nice income for the Pakistanis and a convenient playground for the wealthy. I don't know how true this number is but one thing's for certain: wealthy Sheikhs spend a lot of money on entertainment. "Falcons are very interesting birds," Mohamed continued, adding that there are two kinds: One breed that flies fast and another that flies long distances.

"So what is the price of a falcon?" I couldn't help but ask.

"They can be very expensive. A good one can cost $20,000, but pedigrees can cost as much as $250,000."

"Hmmm. So how do you recover $250,000 that has just flown away?" I was curious to know how they get them back after they are released to chase prey.

Mohamed explained that a GPS transmitter is embedded in the tail. Before they are released for the hunt, SUVs on the ground follow the signal being transmitted from the bird. After the falcon hits its flying prey in the air, it drops to the ground with the prey in its claws and stays there until his handler in the SUV recovers the bird and the prey.

"Some don't come back," Mohamed explained.

"Well, it must be something to watch $250,000 fly away!"

He laughed and agreed.

I learned on that memorable flight how certain cultures and habits live on, although often they get modified based on ever changing societal conditions. Sadly, many traditions become commercialized, as in this case of royal falcons flying on commercial jets. But falcons are not the only animals that have become commercialized. Camels have also followed this trend.

RACING CAMELS

I learned about camels while I was growing up in Egypt. I knew they had been key companions of the nomadic Bedouins. I learned that these creatures can handle desert conditions better than any other species, enduring extreme heat while existing without water for days. Interestingly, their long eyelashes and ear hair form a barrier against blowing sand. In addition to being a mode of transportation, the camel's meat, milk, hides and wool are consumed. Nothing goes to waste. I found it somewhat surprising that even camel dung is useful by desert people; it is burned as fuel for cooking and homes are constructed from it.

Daphne with child camel jockeys in Dubai in 1987.

But I'd never thought about camels as racing animals until my time in the Gulf States. In the old nomadic days, camel racing was not a frequent activity in the Bedouin lifestyle; they were preoccupied with surviving the harshness of their lives in the desert. They only time a camel was raced was when a Sheikh bought a new animal and wanted to test its endurance and riding qualities. When oil wealth changed the lives of the Bedouins starting in the 1960s, camels were replaced by motor vehicles. Bedouins became rich and moved to palatial houses in the cities yet camels remained part of the tradition and local culture. When I lived there, it is was not unusual to see camels parked outside expensive villas in Dubai or Abu Dhabi, kept primarily for the rich owners to provide fresh milk for their children and families.

Camels used for sport became more popular in the Middle East starting in the 1960s, as oil wealth began to change the lives of the indigenous population. Unlike sleek racing horses, camels are awkward-looking animals, but they run surprisingly fast. They're fun to watch! I enjoyed going to a number of races when I lived there back in the 1990s. Friday is usually a big day for camel racing (it's like Sunday here). Racetracks are gathering places for people to visit with their families and be entertained by the races. At that time, there was a lot of controversy about the practice of using children under the age of ten as jockeys. Most of the children used as riders at that time were non-Arabs brought in legally from places like Pakistan, Bangladesh and other Southeast Asian countries. Living conditions for these children were terrible. The industry was tainted with corruption until the authorities put an end to it a few years ago. Child riders are now outlawed and modern technology provides the solution. These days, small robots are secured on the back of the camel to deliver commands to the camel during the races, including a small automatic whip that is operated by remote control from the ground.

To this day, camel racing is a big attraction and a multi-million-dol-

My friend, Tom, and me at the Pyramids in Cairo in 1984.

lar enterprise with high purses. CNN recently reported that the purchase price for a winning camel is more than $2 million. Training and maintaining these camels is also an expensive proposition—which is why only the wealthy continue to own, train and race camels in the Gulf States.

FOLLOW THE SHEIKH!

Weddings in Abu Dhabi, Dubai and Saudi Arabia are different from western weddings, not just religiously but also how the reception is presented. According to local customs, during the ceremony and the reception that follows, male and female guests are kept separate, so typically two wedding celebrations occur at the same time but at different venues. For this reason, when Salem, a good friend of mine from a prominent family in Dubai, had a son who was getting married in the late 1980s, only me and my son, Nick, who was 22 at the time, were invited to attend the reception. Salem's son was marrying the granddaughter of one of the local sheikhs. He was very proud that the family was able to arrange this important wedding. (Marriages are still arranged there today).

It was an elegant affair with hundreds of guests in the ballroom of the Intercontinental Hotel in Dubai. We properly identified our table and sat down with the other male guests. The food was prominently displayed on each table and it looked incredibly delicious. At the center was a full lamb roast, a huge chunk of roasted camel meat, a large tray of rice and twenty or more side dishes of Lebanese and local delicacies. We were instructed to wait for a special guest to arrive before dining. The guest of honor was the grandfather of the bride, and a very prominent sheikh. Thirty minutes passed with no sheikh in sight. That's a long time to wait when you're salivating at all the delicacies displayed in front of your eyes, but we dared not touch anything.

After an hour of our stomachs growling, the sheikh finally arrived in a hurry, followed by his entourage. We watched him with great anticipation and relief that we finally got to have our meal. Well, we were mistaken. The sheikh sat down at the head table and everyone followed his example. Our joy only lasted a few minutes. He got up, said a few words then exited the ballroom with his entourage scurrying behind him.

"What just happened?" I asked the fellow sitting next to me.

"The sheikh probably has another reception or appointment to attend," he replied.

Nick was stunned, and so was I.

"Dad, I'm starving. What now?" he asked.

"Let's wait another minute and see what happens."

A few minutes passed. Many of the guests began to get up from their seats.

"We cannot eat unless the sheikh eats," the man to my left explained.

"Since the sheikh left, we have to follow him out."

Now every guest was exiting the ballroom.

"Dad, I'm not leaving," Nick announced. "I'm going to stay here and when everybody leaves, let's eat, okay?"

"Why don't we take some food with us and eat in the car as we drive back to Abu Dhabi?" I suggested. And with that, we grabbed some food and followed the crowd out of the dining hall.

"What are you going to do with all of this food?" I asked one of the waiters as we were leaving.

"We will distribute it to the poor people," he informed us.

We were glad that at least the food was not going to be wasted.

BRIDGING EAST AND WEST

In all of my years working and living in the Middle East, I had a good understanding of the local culture. As I mentioned earlier, I learned to speak Arabic, a big advantage while living in Arab countries. I quickly and easily made lasting friendships. Remember my story about the policeman at the palace who wanted to take us to jail and ended up trusting me enough to hold my hand (the ultimate sign of friendship) in the marketplace? I connected easily with people, which helped me navigate through bureaucracies and government institutions.

In general terms, Saudis, Kuwaitis, the Emirates, the people in Oman and other places in the region do not share their private lives with Westerners so in general they tend to keep business and personal interactions separate. But I had this ability to understand their culture and communicate in their language—not only spoken language but to their needs. I had a knack for understanding what they needed to feel comfortable both with me and in any given situation. In my years in the region, I developed a few personal friendships and got to meet their wives and children—something that does not happen very often.

I humbly say that one of my professional strengths has been the ability to negotiate successfully. I got things done in very difficult situations. I would say that my children have picked up some of that same trait. Both of my children are good people, with genuine empathy for humanity.

Nicholas took after me and became a diplomat. He joined the United Nations and has moved around the organization in key executive positions. After spending thirteen years in Geneva with the International Organization for Migration, Nick is presently assigned to the UN African Headquarters in Nairobi, Kenya as the Regional Ombudsman and Conflict Resolution Officer. I hear from his colleagues a lot of good reports about his work and how he has helped many people with their lives and careers.

Daphne is also very sensitive to foreign cultures and to people in general. Her contributions as a teacher in Hawaii have been described to me by her superiors as "excellent performance and dedication." I share more about my children later in the book.

I'm sure that their children, my grandkids, will pick up some of this same personality and ability. This gives me a sense of gratification since I want my legacy to be passing onto future generations the rich experiences and strong values that my parents and grandparents instilled in me. It is the ultimate reward for a father.

PART FOUR

A New Life After Retirement

9

A New Career in Academia

After almost a dozen years overseas, we were ready to return home to the States—and circumstances within the company offered me an opportunity to make that happen. As I said earlier, my goal was to retire from Exxon in my late fifties. I felt that the timing to make this happen had almost arrived. The company's offer to relocate me back home opened the door for the ultimate next step: retirement.

In 1996, after eleven years in Abu Dhabi, Exxon decided to reorganize their activities again and transfer me back to headquarters. The theory behind this decision was to cut cost by eliminating the office in Abu Dhabi and run the business from New Jersey. The fact that I had streamlined the operations in the Middle East and established commercial arrangements with all the producers in that region made the decision easier. The transfer had to be done carefully, as my government contacts in the Middle East did not like to see changes of people with whom they had developed strong relationships over the years.

The first day back in the office, I looked around at my co-workers. I couldn't help but notice that at age fifty-eight, I was one of the oldest people in the room. Many of my colleagues had either retired or left the company. In those first few weeks back in the States, I also came to realize that Corporate America had changed during my time overseas. After having a free hand to run things in Abu Dhabi, now I found myself in a very structured and highly competitive environment. It had become much leaner and—yes, younger.

So two weeks after transferring back to New Jersey, I asked for an early retirement. At first my announcement shocked many people in the company, but for me it was an easy decision. I was on target with my career early retirement goal and comfortable with what lied ahead for me. Now I had to convince the company that this was in the best interest of both parties. I wanted out at a time when the company was reducing staff and cutting costs. They were concerned about continuity and any disruptions that my departure may cause with our suppliers and business partners. I assured them that I would help to make the transition smooth and seamless. I was able to negotiate a nice exit package that ensured Demi and me a comfortable retirement.

The company organized a wonderful retirement party for me. The reception was held at a nice resort in New Jersey where I invited all the people I had worked with for so many years. It was an emotional evening, but after that day in September 1996, I've never looked back. Offers from other oil and trading companies came in as they were head-hunting to fill high-level positions but I declined all of them. I wanted to continue working but I wished to do something outside the oil industry.

In the meantime, we had moved back into our house in Old Tappan. Daphne was now out of college and working in Hawaii as a teacher. Nicholas was on his way to Geneva, Switzerland to join the International Organization for Migration. Demi and I decided that it was time for us to do more recreational travel and play more golf. Naturally, we visited Geneva and Hawaii often to spend time with our children. One of my friends used to jokingly say: "George has made a good choice placing his kids in nice places so he can go and visit them anytime he wants." The fact of the matter is that my children made their own decisions, and Demi and I respected and admired their choices—and yes, got the benefit of traveling to interesting and exotic locales to visit them often.

FROM BUSINESSMAN TO VISITING SCHOLAR

After a while, however, travel and golf was not enough to satisfy me. I wanted to do something intellectually challenging and perhaps add some value to society and the people around me. After a fair amount of soul searching and reflection, I decided to become an executive coach. In this role, I could apply my experience and new training to help young executives achieve their goals and plan their careers.

I obtained my certificate as an executive coach in 2003 and that same year, with Daphne's help (she introduced me to program director Nicholas Barker), I was invited by the East West Center at the University of Hawaii in Honolulu to be a visiting scholar. As such, I would conduct research on assessment tools for leadership development in Asian cultures. I spent the next few winters returning to Hawaii. I spent four months each year in Honolulu doing research, teaching and coaching young leaders from more than a dozen countries who were participating in a leadership development program at the university. This program was very successful and hundreds of students from various countries went through it over a period of several years. The following column that I wrote provides a good overview of the program and my role. This was published in the editorial section of the *Honolulu Star Bulletin Newspaper* on June 6, 2004:

COACHING FUTURE LEADERS TO CREATE
A BETTER WORLD

Anyone tempted to feel uneasy when contemplating the next generation of leaders in the Asia Pacific region can breathe easier. My optimism is based on a remarkable experience I have had working with students in the innovative Asia Pacific Leadership Program at the East West Center in Honolulu at the University of Hawaii.

The need to understand other cultures and how to manage cultural diversity is particularly important for leadership development in a post-September 11, constantly evolving and dangerous world. The Asia Pacific leadership program, funded by the Freeman Foundation, fills this need by developing future leaders through personal coaching as they learn leadership skills and theories in a cross-cultural setting.

I was fortunate to be part of this program in 2002 and 2003. The students came from faraway places like Bhutan, Mongolia, Indonesia, China, Tonga, Western Samoa, Nepal and Uzbekistan, as well as the United States, spending nine months at the East West Center.

They ranged in ages from 22-42 years old; included were a doctor from Myanmar, business executives from China, an American Harvard graduate in the foreign service, and a social worker from Thailand. Most had master's degrees and some had completed their doctoral degrees.

They found that adjusting to a new culture was somewhat softened by being in Hawaii with this multi-cultural society and ideal weather. One of their most valuable experiences was sharing their cultures and impressions with one another.

The program's mission was to create a network of leaders from the United States, Asia and the Pacific who are familiar with the region and are trained to exercise leadership for the well being of the countries and people of the region.

My role, through personal coaching, was to facilitate their self-discovery—in effect, to help them achieve what matters most to them. They were challenged to focus on approaches to conflict resolution within different cultures. The students were challenged to look into the future and predict the long-term impacts of their actions.

Gender often plays a part in the coaching process. One young woman from Southeast Asia was moved to tears of frustrations once she identified her personal values and realized they were in direct conflict with her culture. As a result of our conversations, she realized that she could take what she had learned and apply it selectively to her own country to benefit her people. She came up with the idea to go back and start a home for elderly people.

Students felt safe to explore issues and talk openly about their dreams, lives and plans. I listened to their needs, acted as a sounding board and helped them discover options and solutions. Students were encouraged to share what was already working for them. People move forward easier and faster when they acknowledge what is working rather than trying to fix what is not working. After validating their visions by discovering what was ideally right for them and what would make it more right, we explored what was not quite right yet. This process provided a reminder for them to look at options in life from a positive perspective.

We also explored the value of celebrating small things. This concept was revolutionary to some students from Asia, where hard work and achievement are valued over personal gratification. They discover that celebrating small things and daily accomplishments can be an energy booster.

Other topics included decision-making, managing procrastination and exploring their curiosity as a learning tool.

Based on responses students provided, it appeared that the coaching model worked well.

One student wrote: "The program has really opened my eyes to the world. I thoroughly enjoyed the coaching session because it was the first time I actually allotted time to sit down and have someone listen to my career aspirations, qualms and goals."

Program Director Nicholas Barker noted that students reacted to coaching in different ways, applying lessons learned to make life changes. "In certain cases," Barker said, "the impact was dramatic to behold."

My confidence in the leadership of tomorrow extends beyond the students themselves. By helping them discover, define and ultimately achieve what matters most to them, we are helping nations do the same.

MEETING OF THE MASTERMINDS

In 1999, I attended a coaching seminar in Las Vegas organized by the late Thomas Leonard, a prolific and world-recognized professional coach. While in Las Vegas, I met Karim, a Lebanese-American real estate coach. We became friends and met outside the formal sessions of the conference to share stories of our lives in the Middle East.

In one of those meetings, Karim asked if I would be interested in joining a mastermind group that he was organizing. He explained the concept of this group, which was very simple: "People get invited to join a virtual group where two or more persons meet in harmony for one hour once a month with a common purpose to share experiences education and support."

Karim had formed a few of these groups over the years and the ideal number of participants is less than ten people. I liked the idea and joined the group. I was asked to introduce one other person to join the group. I chose Sharon Eakes, a psychologist and a remarkable executive coach from Pittsburgh, Pennsylvania.

Our initial group of six began to meet in 2000. Over the next four years, three people dropped out for various reasons, including health issues. The remaining group consisted of me, Sharon and Hugh Leonard, an ex-Catholic priest, now a management consultant and executive coach who lives in Los Angeles. We continue to meet by phone once a month for a total of fifteen years. We discuss everything from politics and religion to ethics and world events. We often sought support from each other when needed.

I wanted to devote a page in my book to this group because my experiences with these two friends has been invaluable. In addition to sharing knowledge and our diverse backgrounds, they have been there when I needed them in my darkest hours. It has been comforting to go to them for advice and support with personal and family challenges. Their input and understanding has helped me enormously in finding solutions and developing alternative plans in my life.

There is an African proverb that says, " If you want to go fast, go alone. If you want to go far, go together." This summarizes beautifully what my mastermind group has meant to me.

ENJOYING THE ISLANDS

Of course, my post-retirement wasn't all work and no play. I now had time to enjoy more of the things that I may not have had enough time to do when I was focused on my career at Exxon.

Spending winters in Hawaii also gave me the opportunity to spend time with Daphne, who had earned a master's degree at Stanford University in California in1998 and was teaching at Iolani, a prestigious private school in Honolulu. Hawaii is extraordinary. It's as beautiful as people describe it. The islands are laced with natural beauty and history. It has the most beautiful golf courses in the world—and I don't say that lightly because over the years, Demi and I have played on some of the most prestigious courses in the world: Harbour Town Golf Links in Hilton Head, Dunes Golf Club in South Carolina, Ocean Reef in Key Largo and many more. So we added to our list the magnificent Wailae course in Honolulu, where the annual SONY tournament takes place.

We also enjoyed watching the surfers take on big waves—seemingly with no fear or concern about their safety. The north shore of Oahu, with the gigantic waves breaking on the beach, was something to watch with awe. No words can describe the power of these waves and how daring some surfers are doing aerials and "shooting the curl." It was an

Daphne at the NaPali Coast in Kauai in 1995.

amazing experience to get to know some of them and talk to them about their passion for surfing. In February, when the surf is at its best, many surfers would come from far away places just to hang ten. Some lived on the beach in their own surfer culture.

We also visited the big island in Hawaii several times. It's really amazing with its many different (six, I think) ecosystems—from desert, to mountains, to tropical beaches. One of the most spectacular sites is the volcano of Kilauea. It is the most active and most visited in the world today. During one of our visits, the volcano was active and lava was flowing freely from the top all the way down into the sea. It looked like a red glowing river, flowing right into the ocean, where it suddenly solidifies. Truly stunning! The more lava flows, the more the island grows every day. I was so fascinated by this natural phenomenon that I walked too close to the flowing fluid and burned my shoes! I could feel

Family reunion on the NaPali Coast of Hawaii in 1995.

the heat radiating from the hot soil under my feet. It can be dangerous and even fatal. In May 2018, for instance, Kilauea erupted and created a vast ash cloud visible from space. The spewing lava destroyed homes and property.

Daphne stayed in Hawaii for about eleven years, loving every day of it. In 2005, she decided to relocate back to New York to launch a new career in the business world, as professional growth opportunities were limited in Hawaii (more about her life in New York follows later.) Of course, we were delighted that she is now near us and we can see her often and share precious moments with her. The circle has now closed but we sure enjoyed Hawaii while we had the chance.

10

Our Growing Family

The years continued to pass while our children enjoyed bachelor lives with no signs of them settling down. They were in their mid- to late-thirties and we had almost given up any hope that we were going to see grandchildren soon, if at all.

Well, be careful what you wish for because one day, events began to happen fast! In a period of three years, we had two weddings and two new granddaughters. I can say to those aspiring grandparents who have given up waiting (we know a few): Don't despair, it will happen!

NICHOLAS AND FAMILY

In 1988, Nicholas graduated from Colgate University in Hamilton, New York with a bachelor of arts degree in English literature. In 1992, he earned a law degree from Fordham Law School in New York City. The whole family attended the graduation ceremony at the Lincoln Center where Fordham Law School was located. It was an emotional event for the whole family; my mother was there, along with my brother and his wife Paula, Daphne and, of course, Demi and me. We could not hide our proud and joyous emotions when Nicholas was presented with his juris doctorate by the dean of the law school. It was especially a proud day for my mother to witness how far her grandchildren had come from the humble days of their grandparents in Egypt and their great-grandparents

Nicholas' graduation from Fordham Law School in New York in 1992.

in Smyrna and Sinop.

In 2000, Nicholas joined the International Organization of Migration (IOM) in Geneva, Switzerland and a few years later he met Katherine from South Africa, who also worked for the same organization in Geneva. One night in 2007 at two o'clock in the morning, while visiting him in Geneva, Nicholas told his mother that he was going to marry Katherine. Just like that!

They were married in Durban, South Africa in August 2008, Katherine's native hometown and where her family lives. The wedding consisted of two religious ceremonies: The main ceremony was at the Greek Orthodox Church in Durban; a second one took place in the Anglican Church. The reception was held in a beautiful setting in the community where Katherine's three sisters, their husbands, nieces, nephews and parents live. Many of their friends and colleagues flew from Europe and the United States to be with Nicholas and Katherine on their special day. Daphne and her fiancé Chris (more about him in a minute) flew from

Daphne exchanges the crowns at Nicholas' and Katherine's wedding in Durban, South Africa in 2008.

New York to attend the event. It was quite a day to remember!

In the Greek Orthodox Church, the crowning of the bride and the groom is the highlight of the Sacrament of Holy Matrimony. After the priest blessed the two crowns, the koumbara in this case, Daphne interchanged the crowns three times as a witness to sealing the union. It was a beautiful feeling to watch our children bonding and celebrating the union of Nicholas and Katherine.

Soon after the wedding, Katherine was promoted to a high-level position with the United Nations in Vienna, Austria, and the family relocated there. Nick and Katherine rented a beautiful house on the outskirts of Vienna overlooking the Danube River and the breathtaking Austrian countryside. About a year later, in July 2009, our first granddaughter, Penelope was born. Now we had more than one reason to visit them in Austria, and so we did! We really loved Vienna, with its rich history and excellent cuisine. Among its many sites, I particularly enjoyed watching the Lipizzan stallions, where horses and man in perfect riding harmony exhibited skills and grace. Another place high on my list was the Schonbrunn Palace, the former summer imperial residence.

Nicholas and Katherine with nieces Erin and Katie in front of the Greek Orthodox Church in Durban.

While all of these wonderful changes were happening in their lives, Nicholas was offered a high-level position with the UN as Regional Ombudsman for Africa in Nairobi, Kenya. So when Penelope was one year old, the family relocated again to Nairobi. In the summer of 2011, we visited Nicholas and Katherine in Nairobi. Penny was two, old enough to travel with us and visit the Fairmont Mount Kenya Safari Club with magnificent views of Mount Kenya. We stayed one month in Kenya and spent time with our granddaughter, Nicholas and Katherine at their home, as well as travelling and visiting national parks. It was a memorable vacation for all of us.

In 2012, during the last month of Katherine's pregnancy with their second child, Abigail, she decided to give birth in South Africa to be near her family for this special event. Abigail was born in Capetown in July 2012. As of this writing, Nicholas and his family still reside in Nairobi.

DAPHNE AND FAMILY

After graduating from Barnard College in Manhattan in 1992 with a

Daphne with her Yiayia at her graduation from Columbia University in New York City in 1992.

bachelor of arts degree in environmental science, Daphne worked for an environmental nonprofit in New York City for two years.

In 1994, she made the decision to relocate to Honolulu, Hawaii to work for another environmental organization called Earthtrust. At that time, opportunities for a career in Hawaii in environmental sciences were limited. After rethinking her options and interests, she decided that she really wanted to teach. Soon enough, she landed a teaching job at a small Buddhist-affiliated school called Hongwanji Mission School in Honolulu. After one summer teaching second graders, she was offered a full-time position at a special needs school called ASSETS. There she taught seventh through ninth graders for two years then decided to pursue a master's degree in education. She was accepted to Stanford University's School of Education in California and received this degree in 1998.

After graduation, Daphne returned to Hawaii to teach at Iolani Prep School in Honolulu. After eleven great years of professional advancement, surf, sun and falling in love with the Hawaiian culture, she moved back to New York in 2005 to launch a new career in the business world. She joined a healthcare recruitment company called PPR Talent Management based out of Jacksonville, Florida. In 2007, she joined their leadership team and founded their Education Services Division. In a couple of years, Daphne grew that division to the most profitable division in PPR! At the time, she was the only remote employee working from New York. Daphne lived in Tribeca and enjoyed its diversity and endless options—from museums and parks to bars and theaters. She was always in motion in New York! Daphne thrived in this venue change both professionally and with friends and family.

In 2007, during a weekend visit in the Hamptons with her friend Tina, Daphne met Chris and within six months they were engaged. Chris had grown up in East Hampton and had established a successful insurance business there; so it made perfect sense to reside in Sag Harbor on Long Island where they've made their home. In August 2008, six months after Nicholas and Katherine's wedding, Daphne and Chris were married in the Greek Orthodox Cathedral in New York City (the same church that Demi and I were

138

married in 45 years earlier). Daphne looked stunning in her elegant yet simple wedding dress. Walking her down the aisle of this gorgeous cathedral

Proud dad walking the bride down the aisle at the Greek Orthodox Cathedral in New York City in 2008.

was a moment of pride, emotion and admiration for my little girl who was not little anymore. It was one of the happiest days of my life.

Demi and I hosted an elegant wedding reception at the Yale Club in New York City with 200 guests joining us from every corner of the world. In fact, every third person in that ballroom was from a place outside the New York area, which was a testament to Daphne's global

Daphne and Chris' wedding ceremony with Eleni exchanging the crowns.

reach. I am sure my mom (who had passed in 1993) was there in spirit showering her granddaughter with blessings and love.

One year later, Daphne and Chris gave us our second granddaughter, Zoe, and in 2012, Maya was born. With two babies, Daphne left PPR to be at home with the children until they were school age. In the summer of 2018, she returned to work by launching her own Educational Services Company. When she asked me to help her out with the administrative part of setting up the LLC (Limited Liability Corp) and other business aspects of her new venture, I was more than happy to jump in and give her a hand.

OUR FOUR GRANDDAUGHTERS

So now Demi and I are totally enjoying being grandparents to our four beautiful granddaughters. As of this writing, Penelope (Penny) is nine-and-a-half years old, Zoe is nine, and Maya and Abigail (Abby) are six-and-a-half (yes, they are only one month apart).

Because Penelope and Abby live in Nairobi, we don't get to see them as often as Zoe and Maya. Unfortunately, the distance between Nairobi and Sag Harbor is 7,000 miles but the girls get to see each other at least a couple of times a year in New York, Sag Harbor or Greece. The whole family enjoys these visits and the time we spend together with the girls.

All four girls love animals. (I wonder where they inherited that propensity?) Penelope and Abby have a large Rhodesian Ridgeback named Zuri. The girls also have in common a love of horses. Maya helped the staff to take care of the horses at the Green School, a preschool facility not too far from their house that she attend when she was younger. She fed the horses and looked after them. Penelope also loves to take care and ride horses in Nairobi. Her favorite is a horse named Prince. Abby also rides a horse named Gold. Zoe goes horseback riding in Montauk in the Hamptons with her friends. Last year, Penelope was elected to be the third-grade animal keeper at her school in Nairobi; she took care of a hamster named Buzz. This year in the fourth grade, their animal kingdom expanded with the introduction of a hamster named Snow Ball, three fish and an apple snail that keeps the fish company.

The girls enjoy other interests besides animals. Abby is the mathematician in the family, and she likes to swim and ice skate. She and her sister love to read. In fact, Penelope is an excellent reader, well advanced for her age.

I know I am bragging now but I will add that my granddaughters are good at sports, as well. Penelope and Abby take tennis lessons in Nairobi. Zoe and Maya also play tennis and take lessons at the Devon Yacht Club in Amangassett. They love the game, and they're improving every day. Zoe and Maya love to sail. Zoe is an excellent sailor! She now can sail the sunfish and the Optimist class boats on her own.

Swimming is also a favorite pastime that the four girls share. Penelope and Abby take swimming lessons in Nairobi. Zoe and Maya swim at the Devon Yacht Club and in Papou's (my) swimming pool in East Hampton. Their home in Sag Harbor has a swimming pool so they have plenty of opportunities to be in the water all summer. Zoe also joined the swimming team at the YMCA in East Hampton and has done very well in swim competitions.

We also have musicians in the family. Penelope plays the violin.

Zoe, Abby, Maya and Penny at a church festival in Southampton in 2018.

Maya likes to sing and plays the piano. Zoe likes to sing and has taken voice lessons; she has already performed in front of her school and in private recitals.

FAMILY REUNIONS AROUND THE WORLD

It's always a treat when the entire family can be in the same place at the same time. Christmas of 2016 was special for us. Nicholas and his family joined us in the Hamptons to celebrate the holidays and New Year together. We took the girls to New York City and did the typical touristy things: we visited the Empire State Building, Radio City Hall, Central Park, The Metropolitan Museum and many more attractions. Back in Sag Harbor, the four girls went ice skating together. During the visit, Penelope and Abby saw snow for the first time in their lives. They loved creating their first snowman.

In the summer of 2017, we all met in Greece and rented a large beachfront villa on the island of Naxos in the Aegean Sea. It was ten memorable days together. Naxos is one of the biggest Greek Islands. It's famous for its natural beauty but also for potatoes and dairy products, particularly cheese. It combines pristine sandy beaches and rugged mountains. Our villa had a swimming pool so between the sea and the pool, the girls got to play in the water for hours. We also enjoyed horseback riding, huge water slides at a local water park, and of course sampled delicious Greek dishes in traditional *tavernas*. Both the youngsters and us adults were kept busy and happy during this great vacation under the blue skies of Greece. I was a happy man watching all of my family enjoying together the best that Greece has to offer: the sea, perfect weather, hospitality, cuisine, culture and history.

In the summer of 2018, we again had our reunion in New York. Nicholas and his family spent three weeks with us in the Hamptons. Zoe and Maya were the most gracious hosts and made sure their cousins Penelope and Abigail had a good time. The Hamptons offer so many things for the kids to do in warmer months: pristine beaches, horseback riding and swimming. It was a happy time for all of us, especially watching Penny, Zoe, Maya and Abby play together. As a grandparent, it doesn't get any better than that.

Demi and I are blessed to have a close bond with our granddaughters. We love them because of who they are: special, loving, smart and witty. I love to hear what they have to say but also how they say it. To that point, I'd like to share what they wrote about their Yiayia (Demi) on her 77th birthday.

Zoe and Maya:

-I love how you always say "I love you."
-I am so grateful that I have you.
-I love how you always hug me very tight.
-I love spending time with you.
-I'd be lost without your help.
-I still can't believe you were 18 when you came to America.
-You make the best *melomakarona* [Greek sweets].
-I hope to be as smart as you one day.
-I love how you call me every day.
-I love listening to your stories about Greek mythology.
-I love your face and heart.
-Thank you or being the best grandma ever.

Penny and Abby:

-I like the way you compliment us and says we are so pretty.
-You make very good *bougatsa* [salty Greek pastry].
-You help us when we are hurt.
-I like how you keep Greek traditions.
-I like when you say "maybe tomorrow" if we can't do something that day.
-I like how you bake blueberry waffles.
-I like how you hug us.
-I like that you are always happy when we are there.

11

Reflecting on Our Family's Culture and History

Part of what I'd like to pass onto my grandchildren is a sense of the history and deep roots of our family's ethnicity as Greeks. Knowing one's cultural background and what one's ancestors endured—both the pain and the glory—gives context to one's life and sense of belonging.

In these years since I've been retired, I've finally had a chance to work on researching and compiling information about our ancestry. While this memoir spans five generations of my family history covering the period from the mid-19th Century to the year 2018 (about 150 years), I was unfortunately not able to find any oral or written records dating back further, but I feel that sharing the history of the Greek culture is akin to sharing my family's story. In this chapter, I've tried to describe geopolitical events and two political leaders who had a significant impact on millions of people, my family members included.

HELLENISTIC CULTURE

Three things attribute to the Hellenistic identity that has connected all Greeks for many centuries, both those living inside and outside the borders of modern Greece: religion (Greek Orthodox), language (Greek) and, of course, heritage.

Over the years, I've often been asked why I say I'm Greek if my family is from Egypt. "You should be Egyptian and not Greek," is a typical comment. (I have addressed my answer to this question in Chapter One.) The trajectory of Greek history is long and rich and is covered by scholars in many volumes of books. Here I want to briefly review the significant role Greeks of the diaspora played not only in creating a new nation but contributing to its survival after gaining independence.

The Ottomans, or "Turks", under Sultan Bayezid I, began their occupation of Greece in 1397, capturing the cities of Thessaloniki and Athens, and the rest of Peloponnese in the south. It took the Turks nearly 40 years to completely occupy the Greek peninsula. At the time of the fall of Constantinople on May 29, 1453, most of the peninsula was ruled by the Turks. As the Turks ruled over the Greeks, they were granted very limited rights. The Greeks didn't take this occupation lying down; they rose many times against the Turks but were defeated every time.

The year 1821 marked the birth of modern Greece. On March 25 of that year, the Greeks were in open revolt against the Ottomans, thereby sparking the Greek War of Independence after nearly 400 years of occupation under the Ottoman Empire. This war raged on for a decade until the Greek fighters fiercely won Greece's independence from the Turks.

The idea for and initial organization of the 1821 War of Independence is largely attributed to three prominent Greeks: Nicholas Skoutas, Emmanuil Xanthos and Athanasios Tsakalov. These men came together in 1814 in Odessa to decide on the organization of a secret society in free masonic style. They named it Filiki Eteria, or Society of Friends. Their purpose was to unite all Greeks into one army to overthrow Turkish rule. By early 1821, thousands of prominent Greeks from Greek communities abroad had joined the society, including Russian consuls, Ottoman officials, revolutionary Serbs and others. Two other prominent members of the organization included:

- **Alexandros Ypsilantis,** a senior officer in the Imperial Russian cavalry and general and commander of the 1st brigade of Hussars. He also served as aide-de-camp of Tsar Alexander I. He assumed leadership of Filiki Eteria in 1820.

- **Rigas Ferreos,** a Greek writer and political thinker who lived in Bucharest and later became secretary to Ypsilantis.

After Greece's successful war against the Turks, many Greeks of the diaspora continued to help the new nation financially and in other ways to meet the challenges ahead. Greeks from Egypt led the charge, helping modern Greece in significant ways by providing large financial help to a struggling nation. I will mention here only a few names among many:

- **George Averoff** (1815-1899). A prominent businessman in Egypt, he played a key role in banking, transportation and Egyptian agriculture. He founded the Military Academy in Athens and the Agricultural School in Larissa. Averoff financed with his own money the construction of the battleship "Averoff."

- **Emmanuel Benakis** (1843-1929). He managed large estates of cotton in Egypt and was a close friend of the Greek Prime Minister Elefterios Venizelos. Benakis made significant contributions in founding Greek hospitals. A famous museum in Athens bears his name, as do other public institution in Greece and Egypt.

- **Michael Tositsas** (1787 1856). With his brother and sons they were a prominent family and benefactors in the Greek community in Alexandria and Greece. They were founders of hospitals and schools in Alexandria and Greece. Tositsas was one of the most powerful landowners in Egypt and is generally regarded as the father of Hellenism of Egypt.

There were many more Greeks from Egypt who donated personal wealth to help Greece build its public institutions, thus making it possible for the new nation to survive. The historical contributions of these individuals are beyond the scope of this book; however, an excellent treatise of this subject is covered in Manolis Yialourakis' book, *Egypt of the Hellens,* published in 1967 in Greek.

REFUGEES AND IMMIGRANTS

From the early part of the 19th Century through the 1960s, Greece received large waves of refugees from Turkey and Egypt. The country struggled to absorb such a large influx of people, particularly from Turkey. Modern Greece had only gained independence seventy years prior and during that time, it experienced many growing pains, including political instability, economic crises and wars.

During that time period, various geopolitical events resulted in the uprooting of a large Greek populace from Asia Minor and Egypt after thousands of years of presence there. The majority became refugees in Greece and a few sought new homes in America, Australia and elsewhere (including members of my family).

Two political leaders were mainly responsible for the persecutions, massacres and expulsions of the Greeks from Turkey (Asia Minor) and Egypt. In doing so, they had a profound impact on the lives of millions of people. The first leader was Kamal Ataturk (1881-1938), an army officer who founded the Republic of Turkey out of the ruins of the Ottoman Empire. His policies affected Greek (and Armenian) Christians. According to Wikipedia, their tragedy is referred to as the Greek Genocide. Wikipedia estimates that 1.5 million Greeks were expelled and repatriated back to their homeland; many others were massacred by Ataturk's military and civilian forces. The other leader was Gamal Abdul Nasser (1918-1970), who overthrew King Farouk in 1952 and took control of Egypt. His land reforms and Pan Arab socialist policies resulted in the expulsion of hundreds of thousands of Europeans, including Greeks living in Egypt. According to the Egyptian Minister of Immigration Nabila Makram Ebeid in an interview with *Ahram Online* in April 2018, the present Greek population in Egypt has been reduced to a mere 5,000 from its peak of 500,000 in the early 1900s.

GREEKS IN EGYPT

After the fall of Constantinople in 1453 and the invasion of the Greek peninsula by the Ottoman Turks, and until Greece's liberation from the Ottomans in 1829, the country was under an oppressive Turkish occupation for almost 400 years. In spite of this long occupation, the Greek heritage was able to remain strong. This is due in great part to the culture, religion and language that kept the country together all those years. Its rich history helped to maintain the Hellenistic roots during and after the occupation. Democracy was born in Greece in an unparalleled epoch of brilliance in literature, philosophy, science, medicine and visual arts, thus making an enormous contribution to Western civilization. The works of the great philosophers Socrates, Plato and Aristotle, and historians like Herodotus and others, have left a lasting influence in the pursuit of knowledge for all generations that have come since.

The period between 1829 and the early 1900s was very difficult for the struggling new nation. For the remainder of the 19th Century, the country was plagued with political turmoil, military coups, wars and economic instability. A very brief summary of highlights from this complex historical period is presented here to give the reader a glimpse into the enormous challenges the young nation faced.

- The year 1829 marked the declaration of the first Hellenic Re public.
- In 1831, the first governor of Greece, Ioannis Kapodistrias, was assassinated.
- In 1833, the great powers declared Greece a kingdom and selected the young Bavarian King Otto to be its leader. The new king struggled for several years to establish his authority and acceptance but he remained unpopular until in 1862. He was deposed and returned to Bavaria, where he died in 1867.
- In 1863, Prince William of Denmark became the new king as George I.
- In 1881, Thessaly became part of Greece.

- The year 1896 marked the opening of the first Olympic Games.
- The Cretan Revolution began in 1897 and the Ottoman Empire declared war on Greece. The Greeks lose the war and agree to create an international administration for Crete.
- In 1910, Elefterios Venizelos was elected Prime Minister.
- By the early 1900s, the Ottoman Empire began to unravel. Egypt, under the rule of the Mohammed Ali Dynasty, enjoyed a kind of autonomy and booming business climate. Immigrants like Greeks were welcomed there until the 1950s. Greeks and Hellenistic culture were present in Egypt for more than 4,000 years.
- In 1919, Greece declared war on Turkey. King Constantine, after initial tactical successes along the coastline of Turkey, pushed his army to the country's interior with the objective of taking Ankara, the capitol. The Greek army was not prepared for an extended campaign and with poor leadership, suffered huge setbacks on the battlefield. The front lines were finally broken by the Turkish forces led by Kamal Ataturk, resulting in a humiliating retreat and the massacre of Greeks by the Turks—particularly in Smyrna, where my father's family lived.

These were very difficult times for Greece. As I mentioned earlier, that's the time when my father's family fled Smyrna and came to Egypt seeking safety and a new home. After the massacre of Greeks and Armenians in Turkey in 1922, most of the Greeks who lived in Turkey were expelled by the Turks and went to Mainland Greece as refugees. Other Greeks decided to move south seeking asylum.

A question I've frequently been asked over the years is why my grandparents came to Egypt in the late 1800s and early 1900s. The simple answer is that they left their homes under duress and not by choice seeking to find a safe place to live. Egypt, at the time, met these conditions. At the end of the 19th Century, waves of immigrants from Greece,

Cyprus and present day Turkey came to Egypt to settle and find work. The resettlement of these people was easy, as Greece and Cyprus were part of the Ottoman Empire, and so was Egypt.

My theory is that in 1922, my father, his family and some friends escaped in a small boat and sailed south. They probably sailed from Smyrna down to Syria then found a way through Lebanon to Egypt; or perhaps they sailed directly to Alexandria. Unfortunately, I have no documentation to substantiate either route. Egypt at that time was under British protection and it was open and friendly to European refugees. Egypt also had a history of large populations of Greeks, Italians and Jews living and prospering there.

I believe that my father's family ended up in Egypt because they probably felt that the conditions for survival were better there than in Greece, which at the time had to absorb the massive exodus of refugees from Turkey. The conditions for those refugees in Greece were not very good. The country was poor and struggling to stand on is own feet after 400 years of brutal Ottoman occupation. In Greece, they were all refugees. After they arrived in Greece, the government had to provide assistance and camps to accommodate them. Most of them ended up in Athens and Thessaloniki. They lived in poverty for a whole generation. The Greeks who relocated from Turkey to Greece blended in and were absorbed gradually into that homogeneous society. They were ethnically the same with the indigenous population and were predominantly Greek Orthodox Christians. On average, they had high educations and they had a big positive impact on the culture and future prosperity of Greece.

For those who went to Egypt, the conditions and the culture were significantly different. The economic conditions there under British protection were favorable. Egypt was in need of educated people with skills. The refugees from Smyrna and other Turkish cities and villages were looking for opportunities to work and for safety. Some probably knew other Greeks who were in Egypt before them. Even though they were refugees, they were able to quickly establish themselves and create safe homes for their families. With higher education and skills they had a competitive advantage versus the indigenous population.

The other important thing to recognize is that they were Europeans of Greek heritage. Egypt was an Arab country with a Muslim majority. The Europeans, including the Greeks who came to Egypt at that time, were mostly Christians and Jews. They retained their ethnic identity for generations, never assimilating into the Arab and Muslim populations. Under British protection, they were able to prosper while retaining their ethnic identity and religion. Up until the Nasser revolution in the early 1950s, prosperous large pockets of ethnic groups of mainly Greeks, Italians, French and Jews could be found in Egypt. Most of them had moved to the top of the economic scale and owned or controlled key industries like agriculture, banking and finance. They were the elite of the Egyptian society yet very few obtained Egyptian citizenship.

My mother's family also came to Egypt for the same reasons. Some of her family members were very successful. Her Uncle Manolis was an established entrepreneur who became very wealthy. He was the first person to bring neon lights to Egypt. I believe he had exclusive rights in the whole country. He built a factory and controlled the manufacturing of the lights and marketing. He married three times. Marcella, his third wife, was the Italian woman who actually lived in the same building with my mother's family and was very close to my mother and taught her Italian. Manolis was also my godfather when I was baptized in the Greek Orthodox Church. Manolis was also a big spender, way ahead of his time. He was a major benefactor of the Monastery of Saint Katherine in the Sinai Peninsula, which he visited often in his flashy red convertible. I was told that he would come and take me in his convertible and ride the streets of Cairo with the top down to the envy of onlookers who happened to be around. My relatives joked by telling stories about him, claiming that the only other two red convertibles in Egypt were owned by King Farouk.

THE PURSUIT OF HAPPINESS

Nasser's rule was not as bloody as Ataturk's but the end result was devastating. Thousands of Greeks who lived in Egypt for generations had to leave with most of them repatriating back to Greece. Some moved to other European countries and Australia. Only a handful, like my brother Takis and me, came to America. We are the fortunate ones. We were welcomed here and we gave back the best we had in return for that opportunity. We are thankful for all of the blessings we have enjoyed as American citizens.

I became an American citizen on May 21, 1968. It was a proud moment for my family and me. My dream came true as I was welcomed to the land of the free. My children and grandchildren are U.S.-born citizens. The American democratic system, despite all its problems, works in an ingenious way. Everybody, regardless of religion, ethnicity or color, blends in this melting pot called America.

As I write these lines, our nation is struggling with immigration issues and a leadership crisis at the top. I am hopeful that our longstanding institutions will survive and that Americans will continue to enjoy the freedom and opportunities inherent in our great nation. We are fortunate to be citizens of a county where everyone is equal under the Constitution of United States of America.

The Declaration of Independence states: "That all people are created equal, that they are endowed by their Creator with certain unalienable Rights, that among these are Life, Liberty, and the Pursuit of Happiness...." But in a society as diverse as ours, it is just as important to remember our roots and family heritage, which was kept alive for so many centuries—more often than not, in the most adverse conditions.

12

A Childhood Dream

One night when I was a child, I had a dream—or, maybe I thought I had a dream and was imagining it all. It went like this: It was the spring of 1922 and I was in my grandfather's house in Smyrna. My father was there also, along with my uncles, aunts and my grandmother.

The atmosphere in the house was tense and I could see fear in my family's faces. People in the house were whispering but I could hear their discussions. The Turkish Army, they whispered, had overrun the last defensive positions of the Greek forces in the interior of the country and were moving towards Smyrna, burning Greek villages on their way. I peered out of the window and could see the harbor of Smyrna just as Marjorie Housepian Dopkin described it in her book, *Smyrna 1922: The Destruction of a City:*

"In spite of the war raging in the interior, life in Smyrna had been unaffected, until the last days of August 1922. The city was the centre of the nation's commercial and agricultural life, and although trade in the interior was diminished, the harbor bustled with traffic, displaying an armada of Allied might. Twenty-one warships; two British battleships, three cruisers and six destroyers; three French cruisers and two destroyers; an Italian cruiser and destroyer; and three American destroyers—the harbor was massed with virtually every sort of vessel that could float, from tiny Levantine caique to massive freighters bearing the flags of all the maritime nations on earth except Greece."

My dream continued and for the next few days I noticed a lot of preparations in the house. My grandfather was giving instructions and all the women were busy packing personal effects. Visitors came to the house, men mostly, and drank coffee, talking in low voices about the latest news. It was all somber but they spoke in a calm manner, the men almost oblivious to the imminent catastrophe, despite reports of massacres and looting in the interior in the twenty-three local newspapers. And then the first wave of Kamal Ataturk's army entered Smyrna. Again, the words of Dopkin capture the scene:

"It was General Marcelle Pasha's celebrated cavalry regiment that appeared in the northern tip of the quay . . . The horsemen loomed high on their horses. Their curved, gleaming sabres drawn and raised in their right hand. On their heads they wore black fezzes emblazoned with the red crescent and star. All Saturday afternoon the infantry followed the cavalry into Smyrna, dressed in a bewildering assortment of uniforms. Some of the men were outfitted in rough khaki, others in American army uniforms, other soldiers wore baggy trousers, crossed bandoliers, and carried an intimidating array of daggers. These troops were referred to as Chettes (irregulars) integrated into Kamal's army."

Morale among the troops was maintained by the desire to loot. Armenian and Greek stores were the first to be looted, and looting soon turned into armed robbery and massacre. That night, as the infantry be gan pouring into the city, my grandfather gathered the family around the fireplace, gave last-minute commands and each member exited the house carrying a few personal pieces of luggage. Before we started walking towards the harbor, grandfather locked the front door of the house, made the sign of the Cross, turned around and never looked back.

We arrived at the quay in darkness, where a caique, a small traditional fishing boat (kaiki) was waiting for us. The Turkish captain and my grandfather exchanged a few words, and as we began boarding the boat, I saw my grandfather hand over to the captain a small bag filled with English gold coins. The captain ordered the children and women to go below. I watched my father and grandfather standing at the stern of the boat watching Smyrna disappearing slowly from our eyes as the caique pulled away from the dock.

Just as the boat was turning around the breakwater of the harbor and before we lost sight of the city, the first buildings began to burn. The destruction of the Smyrna had started.

Then, I woke up. I was at the farm in Egypt. Through the window of my bedroom I could see my father standing under the tall eucalyptus tree in his usual post, talking to his foremen about the daily activities and work. We were home and safe.

FINDING ITHAKA

Throughout my adult life, I regretted that I never asked my father or my aunt how their family escaped from Smyrna and how or when they came to Egypt. They never volunteered to tell me this story. Thinking back, I now realize how painful that experience must have been for them. They just put it all behind them and never looked back, nor did they share it with anyone else.

As for the future generations of my family, I want them to know about our family, our ancestors, our culture and how we got here in America. And now that we are here we should take our civic duties seriously and rise to the call for the public to do what is right for the greater good. Let us be guided by President John F. Kennedy's powerful message: "Ask not what your country can do for you; ask what you can do for your country."

As my granddaughters embark on their life journeys, they will no doubt have many interesting adventures. They will gather knowledge along the way, taste defeats and disappointments, and hopefully experience mostly triumphs. But regardless of the situation at any particular time, my hope is that they will always be guided by three things:

1. Know who you are.
2. Know what you want.
3. Do the best you can.

As for me, this is the final chapter of my long journey. I have lived a good life. I have experienced adventures and new discoveries. I have worked hard and had successes and failures but in the end I'm blessed with a wonderful family and being able to live the American dream. I have witnessed what the Alexandrian Greek poet C. P. Cavafy describes in his poem at the opening of these pages:

". . . mother of pearls and coral, amber, and ebony, sensual perfumes of every kind . . ."

His poem captures perfectly the essence of my story. Ithaka is the name of the island located on the western coast of Greece where Ulysses (Odysseus) was born and to where he returned home after the Trojan War.

Like Ulysses, I too have finally arrived home . . . to my Ithaka.

PART FIVE

My Family's Voices

13

Short Stories:
My Father's Writings

One of my father's few hobbies was his passion to write, mostly short stories about working the land and the lives of the Egyptian peasants. He wrote of real people, toiling the land with their blood and sweat.

Dad's stories were regularly published in the largest Greek language newspaper in Alexandria, *Tachydromos*. I was able to locate and save some of the original papers published between 1948 until the time of his death in 1954. Below are a few of my favorites. I have included the originals in Greek with English translations. Special thanks to Takis and Paula for translating these short stories.

Story #1

A LETTER TO THE EDITOR

Under the Storm

Dear Mr. Sevastopoule,

I have received your article regarding the development of the desert by a Greek Egyptian businessman. You are the only reporter who has visited the vineyards in this area; however, you have neglected to mention Mr. Mourafetlis, a businessman from Cairo, and also Mr. Nicholas Theotocatos' partner. It is indeed a miracle that we were able to develop this arid area and make it one of the best vineyards in Egypt.

We worked very hard and made sacrifices to accomplish our goal notwithstanding financial and personal sacrifices. We love this land and hope for a better day tomorrow. But the most impressive accomplishments are those of the visionary Mr. Pierakos, owner of the Gianaclis Vineyards, who I have the privilege to know personally. Among many other accomplishments and through his personal efforts, he was able to persuade the government to dredge the canal Noubaria thus providing ample supplies of water to irrigate our land. There is also a master plan to extend Noubaria all the way to Alexandra. If one day this ambitious plan is completed, then Mariout, the area known for its large estates and plush homes in Pharaonic times, will be revived again to its old glory.

The development of the area will also offer opportunities for the citizens of Alexandria to visit with their families in Mariout and its vineyards that remind us so much of Greece.

Κάτω άπ' τή θύελλα

Ένα γράμμα

Έλαβα τὸ ἀκόλουθο γράμμα·
«Ἀγαπητὲ κ. Σεβαστόπουλε,
Ἐδιάβασα τὸ χρονογράφημά
σας γιὰ τὴν ἀξιοποίησι τῆς ἐ
ρήμου ἀπὸ Ἕλληνας ἐπιχειρη
ματίας. Αὐτὸς, πράγματι, εἶνε
ὁ Αἰγυπτιώτης Ἕλλην. Εἰσθε
ἴσως ὁ μόνος δημοσιογράφος
ποὺ ἐπεσκέφθη τὴν ἄλλοτε ἐρη
μον περιοχήν μας, ἡ ὁποία σή
μερα ἔχει μεταβληθεῖ εἰς ἀπε
ράντους ἀμπελῶνας καὶ κήπους
ὀπωροφόρων δένδρων.. Παρα
λείψατε μόνον τὸ ὄνομα τοῦ κ.
Κ. Μουφαρετλῆ, βιομηχάνου
ἐκ Καΐρου καὶ οι νιδιοκτήτου τοῦ
κτήματος Θεοτοκάτου.

Ἕνα πραγματικὸ θαῦμα ἔχει
συντελεσθεῖ σὲ διάστημα 8 περί
που ἐτῶν, κατόπιν κόπων καὶ
μόχθων καὶ ὑλικῶν θυσιῶν πολὺ
ἀνωτέρων ἄλλων κτημάτων ἄλ
λων περιοχῶν τῆς Αἰγύπτου.
Κατωρθώσαμεν νὰ ἀξιοποιήσω
μεν — ὅπως γράφετε — τὴν
ἄγονον αὐτὴν γῆν, ἀλλ' αὐτὸ ἐ
γινε χάρις μόνο στὴν ἀκατά
βλητη ἐπιμονὴ καὶ τὴν ἀνεξάν
τλητη ὑπομονὴ τοῦ Ἕλληνος.
διὰ τῆς ἀσκητικῆς ζωῆς ποὺ
διάγομεν, παραμένοντες διαρ
κῶς ἐδῶ καὶ ἐργαζόμενοι σκλη
ρά, μὲ πραγματικὴ ἀφοσίωσι
εἰς τὸν σκοπόν μας. Δὲν ἀπε
βλέψαμεν εἰς ἄμεσα κέρδη. Ὑ
πάρχουν κτήματα τὰ ὁποῖα ὄχι
μόνο δὲν ἀποδίδουν ἀκόμη κέρ
δ'ς, ἀλλὰ κλείνουν τὸν ἰσολογι
σμόν των μὲ ἀρκετὰ σοβαρὸν
πλεόνασμα εἰς τὴν μερίδα τῶν
ἐξόδων. Καὶ ὅμως ἐργαζόμεθα
μὲ τὸν ἴδιον ρυθμὸν δαπανῶν.
μὲ τὴν αὐτὴν ἀγάπην πρὸς τὴν
μητέρα γῆν καὶ μὲ τὴν πεποί
θησιν καὶ τὴν ἐλπίδα εἰς μίαν
καλλιτέραν αὔριον.

Αὐτὰ τὰ ὀλίγα γιὰ μᾶς τοὺς
μικροκτηματίας Ἕλληνας τοῦ
Μαριοὺτ. Τὸ μεγαλείτερον ὅμως
θαῦμα, ἡ μεγαλειτέρα καὶ πλέον
θεώδης ἐπιχείρησις εἶνε τῶν
κτημάτων τοῦ κ. Πιερράκου.
Σ' ἄλλα μέρη ἡ διαφήμισις θὰ
ὠργίαζε. Ἡ μετριοφροσύνη ὅ
μως τοῦ κ. Πιερράκου εἶνε
γνωστή.. Ἐντούτοις, ὅποιος τον

ἐγνώρισε ἀπὸ κοντὰ καὶ παρη
κολούθησε τὴ δημιουργική του
ἐργασία, αὐτὸς μόνο μπορεῖ νὰ
ἐκτιμήση τ' ἀποτελέσματα τῆς
τεσσαρστίας προσπαθείας του.

Στὴ μεγάλη αὐτὴ ἐπιχείρησι
ὀφείλομε κι' ἐμεῖς τὴν ἄνετον
ὕδρευσιν τῶν γαιῶν μας ἀπὸ
τὴν διώρυγα Νουμπαρία. Διότι,
χάρις εἰς τὰς ἀπεράντους ἐκ
τάσεις τῶν ἀμπελώνων Τσανα
κλῆ,. τὸ ὑπουργεῖον τῶν Δημ.
Ἔργων ἐνδιεφέρθη διὰ τὴν Ἐκ
βάθυνσιν τῆς ἐν λόγῳ διώρυ
γος.

Ὑπάρχει ὅμως καὶ τὸ μεγάλο
σχέδιο τῆς διειρύνσεως καὶ
προεκτάσεως τῆς διώρυγος αὐ
τῆς μέχρις Ἀλεξανδρείας. Ἐὰν
τὸ σχέδιον αὐτὸ ἐκτελεσθῆ, τότε
ἡ Μαρεῶτις, ἡ τὸ πάλαι γνω
στὴ περιοχή, μὲ τοὺς ὀνομα
τοὺς τῆς ἀμπελῶνας καὶ τὰς
περικαλλεῖς ἐπαύλεις τῶν μεγι
στάνων, θὰ ξαναζωνταντύση.
Θὰ ξαναζωντανεύση ὅμως σ'
ἕναν καινούργιο ρυθμό, μὲ νεω
τεριστικὰς πλέον μεθόδους διὰ
τὴν ὕδρευσιν, τὴν καλλιέργειαν,
τὴν μεταφοράν κλπ. Καὶ οἱ κά
τοικοι τῆς Ἀλεξανδρείας θὰ
μπορῶσιν νὰ περάσουν τὰς ὥρας
τῆς ἀργίας των στὸ θυγγλαιο
αὐτὸ κλίμα τοῦ Μαριοὺτ, μέσα
σὲ ἀπεράντους ἑλληνικοὺς κή
πους, σὲ μιὰ καθάρια ἀτμόσφαι
ρα. Γιατὶ εἶνε ἀλήθεια ὅ,τι
εἶπαν κάποτε εἰδικοὶ ποὺ ἐπε
σκέφθησαν τὴν Ἐρημο. Ἡ φύ
σις σ' αὐτὴ εἶνε τόσα ἴδια κι'
ἀπαράλλακτη μὲ τὴν ἑλληνικὴ
ρύσι, ὥστε θἄλεγε κανεὶς ὅτι
τρὶν χρόνια καί χρόνια τὸ Μα
ριοὺτ δὲν χωριζόταν ἀπ' τὴν
Ἑλλάδα, ὅτι δὲν ὑπῆρχε ἀνάμε
σά τους ἡ Μεσόγειος κι' ὅτι ἡ
Μαρεῶτις ἦταν ἡ προέκτασις
τῆς ἑλληνικῆς γῆς.

Μὲ πολλὴ ἐκτίμησι
ΝΙΚΟΣ ΘΕΟΤΟΚΑΤΟΣ»

Ἴσως στὰ τελευταῖα λόγια
τοῦ γράμματος αὐτοῦ ὑπάρχει
ἡ ἐξήγησις τῆς ἕλξεως ποὺ
ἐξασκεῖ τὸ Μαριοὺτ στοὺς Ἕλ

Ληνας ἐπιχειρηματίας. Δὲν τοὺς
τραβᾶ μόνο ἡ ἐρημιὰ κι' ὁ ὡ
ραῖος ἀγώνας τῆς ἀξιοποιήσεώς
της. Τοὺς τραβᾶ, μὲ κάποια μυ
στηριώδη δύναμι, κι' ἡ περίερ
γη φύσις της, ἡ ἑλληνικὴ τῆς
φύσις, μὲ τὰ ταπεινὰ ἐκεῖνα κι'
ἀπόκοσμα στολίδια της ποὺ σκε
πάζουν τὴ γῆ κι' ὅταν σαλεύουν
κάτω ἀπ' τὸ μυρωμένο χάδι
τοῦ ἀέρα, φαίνονται σὰν νὰ
χαιρετίζουν τὸν γνώριμό τους
ἀσκητή, τὸν Ἕλληνα ποὺ ἔρχε
ται νὰ τὰ συντροφέψη...

Α. ΣΕΒΑΣΤΟΠΟΥΛΟΣ

YIANNIS' WEDDING

I knew my friend Yiannis from my teenage years. He was fat, bold and very religious. He lived with his mother who had a great influence on him. He was a clerk with a local bank, and his daily dream was to find a girl and marry her. His mother was a nightmare in his private life and she had the last word concerning all wedding proposals for her son.

Finally his mother found a young woman who she felt was the right person for her son. She came from a wealthy family. Her father had agreed to furnish an entire department and give Yiannis a wedding gift of 300 pounds. Yiannis was very happy with his mother's choice and he accepted this beautiful lady as his future wife. Their engagement was announced a couple of weeks later.

A few days before the wedding, Mr. Markos, the father of the bride, received a letter from Yiannis outlining his demands for the wedding:

Dear Father-in-Law,

As the wedding day is approaching rapidly, I feel obligated to tell you now that I have the following demands. a) I expect to receive the dowry of 300 pounds that you promised by Monday of next week. I need this cash to invest in my new company I plan to establish. Details of my new company will be mailed after I launch this new business. b) I expect you buy us a new home, fully furnished. The title of the house would be in my name.

Respectfully,
Yiannis

This letter shocked Mr. Marcus as if lightening had hit him. He showed the letter to his wife and told her how fortunate they where that God had open their eyes early in the game to protect them from the future son-in-law.

"Do you know how much your future son-in-law earns in the bank where he works?" he asked his wife. "Six pounds a month and he was telling us that he earns 12 pounds. If he gives two pounds a month to his crazy mother, and three pounds a month towards rent, that leaves him only one pound for food. He has not stopped asking us this and especially that he wants us to buy him a private home in his name. And let's not forget that he is demanding that he receives his dowry now, so he can invest this money into his new business opportunity before the wedding.

"My dear wife," Mr. Markos said, "this wedding will never take place under these conditions."

The gifts for the groom, including the wedding ring, were returned to the jewelry store. The person who organized the entire affair was very disappointed when she found out that the wedding was canceled. She was going to lose the profit she'd make on the rings and was also very upset that she would also lose her commission on this entire affair.

Many years passed by and Yiannis was still a single man. Every wedding proposal that came along, his mother found a way to sabotage it, and Yiannis continued to be single and lonely. One day his mother died and he was left alone without a single soul to keep him company.

After his mother's death, Yiannis changed completely. He became selfish, arrogant and very difficult to deal with. He told his friends that his goal was to get married and start a family. He took excellent care of himself and tried to look younger, pretending to be wealthy. Although he was 60 years old, he advertised that he was only 45 years old, very wealthy and a good catch for a young lady who was looking for a husband. Eventually, his efforts finally paid off and he succeeded to find a bride. She was a 20-year-old woman from the suburbs who was visiting Cairo with her uncle to attend the feast of St. George.

Yiannis met her in a friend's house and he immediately recognized that this girl was a potential bride. He fell in love with this young woman and he proposed. She was impressed with Yiannis when she realized that he was wealthy and she convinced herself that he was not much older than her. They were married in the Cathedral of St. George with many guests attending the wedding ceremony. It was a rainy day with heavy winds and black clouds in the sky as if nature was sending a warning that this mismatched union was in trouble.

In the first year following the wedding, Yiannis aged at least 20 years. His friends never stop teasing him and made fun of him often by using very derogatory remarks.

One night he returned home early and was shocked to find his wife in their bed with a young man. He stood by the bedroom door for a few minutes and started to cry then he turned around and left his house heartbroken. His body was found the next day floating in the dark waters of the Nile.

Mahdia, 28 April 1949

ΤΑ ΑΠΡΟΟΠΤΑ ΤΗΣ ΖΩΗΣ

ΤΑ ΠΑΝΤΡΟΛΟΓΗΜΑΤΑ ΤΟΥ ΓΙΑΝΝΗ

Γνωστός από τά παιδικά μου χρόνια, κοντόχονδρος, φαλακρός, θρησκόληπτος όσο δέν φαντάζεσθε, μιά τό πιό περίεργο σ' αὐτά πού θά σᾶς διηγηθῶ γιά τήν ζωή τοῦ Γιάννη ήταν ή Μάνα του.

Ὑπάλληλος σέ μιά τράπεζα, τό ὄνειρό του, ή καθημερινή του σκέψις, ήταν ὁ γάμος. Ἡ Μάννα του ὅμως, κέρβερος στήν ἀτομική του ζωή, εἶχε τόν τελευταῖο λόγο σέ κάθε προξενειά πού ἔφεραν γιά τόν γυιό της, καί στό τέλος ἀπετύγχαναν μιά πίσω στήν ἄλλη.

Καί μιά μέρα εὐρέθηκε ή νύφη πού ἔκανε ἐντύπωσι στήν Μάννα τοῦ Γιάννη. Ήταν ὄμμορφη, θά τοῦ ἐπίπλωνε καί τό σπίτι, καί θά τούδινε καί τριακόσιες λίρες μετρητά γιά προῖκα. Κι' ὁ Γιάννης τρελλίνο ἀπ' τήν χαρά του δεχθηκε κι' αὐτός, εἶδε τήν νύφη ἐνθουσιάσθηκε καί σέ λίγο ἔγιναν κι' ἀρραβώνες.

Λίγες μέρες πρίν γίνουν οἱ γάμοι, ὁ κύρ Μάρκος — πατέρας τῆς νύφης — ἔλαβε ἔνα γράμμα ἀπό τόν μέλλοντα γαμβρό του καί ν' ὅ τί τοῦ ἔγραφε.

Σεβαστέ μοι πατέρα
Ἡ ἡμέρα τοῦ γάμων μας πλησιάζει, ὡς ἐκ τούτου θεωρηρῶ καλόν νά σᾶς γνωστοποιήσω τά ἐξῆς.

α) Ζητῶ τήν καταβολήν τῶν τριακοσίων λιρῶν τῆς προικός πού μοῦ ὑπεσχέθητε τό ἀργότερον μεθαύριον καθ' ὅτι πρόκειται νά κανονίσω μίαν ἀτομικήν καί σπουδαίαν ἐπιχείρησιν διά ὁποίαν θά μάθετε ἀργότερον...

— β) Ζητῶ χωριστήν κατοικίαν,

γ) Ἔκλογήν ἐπίπλων τῆς ἀρεσκείας μου καί ἀγοράν αὐτῶν τοῖς μετρητοῖς καταχωρουμένων ἐπ' ὀνόματί μου

Μέ σεβασμόν, ὁ γαμβρός σας
ΓΙΑΝΝΗΣ Κ.....

"Άν ἔπεφτε κεραμιδα στό κεφάλι τοῦ γέρο Μάρκου, δέν θά τόν ἐξαφνιζε τόσο, ὅσο τοῦ γαμβροῦ του τό γράμμα...

— Βρέ γυναῖκα, διάβασε πιῦ'τό δῶ τό γράμμα τοῦ γαμβροῦ σου, καί πές μου ἄν ὁ Θεός δέν μᾶς ἀγιησε, γιατί μᾶς ἄνοιξε τά μάτια ἐγκαίρως. Καί ξεύρεις πόσα περίζει στήν Τράπεζα πού ἐργάζεται ὁ προκομένος; Ἕξη λίρες τόν μήνα, καί μᾶς ἔλεγε δώδεκα. Ζητά αὐτό, ζητά ἐκεῖνο, καί ἐχωριστή κατοικία. Μά δέν μοῦ λές τώρα ἐσύ σάν μυαλωμένη γυναῖκα πού εἶσαι, ὅταν θά δίνη δυό λίρες τόν μήνα στήν θεσσαλαβή τήν Μάννα του κι' τρεῖς τό νοίκι μᾶς κάνουν πέντε, τότε τί θά τοῦ μένουν γιά τροφή; Μιά λίρα! Καί ζητά τήν προῖκα μπροστά γιατί θά κάνη μιά ἐπιχείρησι... "Ότι γυναῖκα. "Εως ἐδῶ καί μή περέκει. Ὁ γάμος αὐτός δέν θά γίνη. Καί δέν ἔγινε.

Τά δῶρα τοῦ γαμβροῦ — δυό δαχτυλιδάκια ἐστάλησαν πίσω, κι' ἡ προξενήτρα ἔφριξε γιά τήν ματαίωση τοῦ γάμου, μιά πού θά ἔχανε τήν μεσιτεία.

Πέρασαν κάμποσα χρόνια ἀκόμη κι' ὁ Γιάννης ἔμενε ἀνύπανδρος. Κάθε φορά πού τοὺβρισκαν νύφη, ἡ μάννα του τόν ἔδοζε κι' ἔγραφε νέους ὅρους νέας ἀπαιτήσεις, πού μιά χαρακτηριστική ἐπιβολή πάνω στό γυιό της τόν κρατοῦσε πάντα αἰχμάλωτο.

Κι' οἱ προξενειές μιά πίσω στήν ἄλλη ἐρανταιωνονταν — Ἔλεγαν μάλιστα οἱ κακές γλῶσσες, πώς ἀπό σκοπό τά ἔκανε αὐτά, γιατί δέν ἤθελε νά τόν παντρέψη.

Καί μιά μέρα πέθανε ἡ μάννα του ἡ χαρά Θανανο κι' ἔμεινε ὁλομόναχος στόν κόσμο.

Τώρα ὁ Γιάννης ἄλλαξε, ἔγινε ἀγνώριστος, ἰδιότροπος, ἐγωιστής, καί τό κυριώτερο, ἄρχισε συστηματικά μ' ὅλα του τά ἐξῆντα χρόνια — τήν καταστρατήγησι τοῦ γήρατος, Καί σέ λίγο ζητοῦσε νύφη. «Θέλω νά ἀποκτήσω οἰκογένεια» ἔλεγε στούς φίλους του. Κι' αὐτοί γελοῦσαν.

Εὐχάτατος ὅμως ἦταν τώρα, ἐξ-ξέδευε. Οἱ προξενήτρες ἄρχισαν τή δουλειά τους. Τόν συνέστηναν γιά πολύ πλούσιο, μόλις σαραντανεντάρη — καί τόσο φαινόντανε..

Καί τό πουλάκι πιάστηκε.

Μιά νέα μόλις εἰκοσι χρονῶν, ἐπαρχιώτισσα εἶχαν ἔλθη μαζί μέ τόν Θεῖον της στήν πρωτεύουσα γιά τήν γιορτή τοῦ "Αη Γιώργη Οἱ γνωριμίες ἔγιναν σ' ἔνα κοινό φιλικό σπίτι, ὅλως τυχαίως... Ὁ Γιάννης εἶδε τή νύφη, τοῦ ἄρεσε καί τήν ἀγάπησε. Τόν εἶδε κι' ἡ νύφη. — ἀφοῦ πρῶτα τῆς γέμισαν τό μυαλό. Πλούσιος εἶνε Ε!... ὅχι καί πολύ μεγάλος. 'Αμέ τί θέλεις παιδάκια πού ξαναβλέπουν μόλις περάση ὁ πρῶτος μήνας τοῦ γάμου.

Κι' ἡ Σάσα συνήνεσε Κι' οἱ γάμοι ἔγιναν μέ ὅλην τήν μεγαλοπρέπειαν πού ἐπιθυμοῦσε ὁ γαμβρός — μιά χειμωνιάτικη καί βροχερή βραδυά — πού νόμιζε κανείς πώς τά στοιχεῖα τῆς φύσεως ἤθελαν νά ματαιώσουν τόν ἀταίριαστον αὐτόν γάμον.

Συμβαίνει πολλές φορές νά εἴμεθα ἄρρωστοι σοβαρά καί ὅμως θέλουμε νά πιστεύουμε πώς εἴμεθα ὑγιεῖς. Γέροι καί νά θεωροῦμε τόν ἑαυτό μας νέα.

Τό ἴδιο ἔπαθε κι' ὁ Γιάννης.

Καί ὅμως ἀπό τήν ἡμέρα πού παντρεύτηκε εἶχε γηράσει κατά εἰκοσι χρόνια. Κι' οἱ φίλοι του πάντα τόν πείραζαν καί πειό τολμηρά.

— Καλή μέρα κύρ Γιάννη, Τι νέα; πότε θά μᾶς ἔλθη ὁ διάδοχος;

— "Ε, πλησιάζει. Στόν δρόμο τὤχουμε. Καί τί σκάνδαλο, πού ὁ κόσμος ἀπό καιρό τό γνώριζε — ξέσπασε. Σέ μιά ἀπρόοπτη ἐπιστροφή στό σπίτι, βρῆκε τήν γυναῖκα του στήν ἀγκαλιά ἐνός νέου. Δέν ἔβγαλε λέξι ἀπό τό στόμα του. Στάθηκε λίγα λεπτά κασφωμένος στήν πόρτα τῆς κρεββατοκάμαρας του κάτι λυγμοί βγῆκαν ἀπό τά στήθη του, καί ἔφυγε πάλι. — ἔγινε ἄφαντος.

Ὁ χαμός του ἦταν μοιραῖος.

Τοῦ ἔραναν ἀπίστευτο αὐτά πού εἶδαν τά μάτια του. Εἶχε τόσην ἐμπιστοσύνη στόν ἑαυτόν του, στάς νεανικούσας δυνάμεις του, καί τόσην βεβαιότητα στήν ἀγνότητα τῆς νέας του γυναικας! Καί προτίμησε τήν ἀφανισμό του μέσα στόν ὑγρό τάφο τοῦ Νείλου.

ΜΑΗDIA 28 'Απριλίου 1949
ΝΙΚΟΣ ΘΕΟΤΟΚΑΤΟΣ

ΕΥΘΥΜΑ ΚΑΙ ΑΝΟΗΤΑ

Ὁ δάσκαλος κάνει μιάν ἐρώτησι σ'

Story # 3

MAHMOUD'S LOVE: FROM THE VILLAGE

I met Mahmoud in one of my regular visits to the area. He was the local railroad station manager in his early twenties with blue eyes. He was a very attractive individual and very successful with the young ladies. When I first met him he was in love with two young girls, Rachel and Rosa. Rachel was working in a women's clothes factory and Rosa was working in the large modeling store for women.

Because of frequent visits with his two girlfriends to his small apartment he owned at the station, he acquired the title of "Don Juan." His relationships with the two young ladies demanded that he would frequently spend a lot of time with each individually until early morning. His dual relationships with the two girlfriends began to cause him some serious problems with his job. One morning, I arrived at my destination on the first train. I immediately noticed unusual activity for the small station at this time of the day. I also observed a serious delay for the train's departure. I felt that something was seriously wrong.

I decided to go to Mahmoud's office to find out what was happening at the railroad station so early in the morning. I found Mahmoud in his office. He told me that after two nights of drinking and having fun he was assigned the night shift. But while on the shift it did not take him long to fall asleep. While he was sleeping, the four o'clock commercial train entered the station going the wrong direction fell off the track and blocked the train I was to travel on. Fortunately, that there were no casualties. Thanks to the connection he enjoyed with the management of the railroad company, he was able to avoid any major punishment or consequences from this accident. He was only charged 15 days penalty from his salary.

Sometime later after the incident, I received a letter from Mahmoud inviting me to his home the following Saturday to tell me something very serious that have happened to him. When I visited him at his home,

I found him very sad and anxious to meet me and talk to me.

"You know how much I love Rachel," he said.

"How about Rosa?" I asked. "You do not love her anymore?"

"I'm not talking about marrying Rosa," he responded. "I am going to marry Rachel."

"Mahmoud," I told him, "you're planning to marry a young lady with a different religion, and the most important obstacle is that you plan to marry her without your father's approval.

"As far as Rachel is concerned," he continued, "she promised me that she will convert to my religion. As far as my father's concern, I am sure that he will forgive me because he loves me very much."

"Mahmoud," I said, "I truly do not agree with the arguments you presented me. Marrying Rachel is the wrong decision and it would complicate your life."

After my discussions with Mahmoud, I concluded that he was so much in love with Rachel that nothing could stop him from marrying her. He was convinced that Rachel loved him and he loved her and he would marry her regardless of her religion, her young age (she was 16 years old) and how poor she was.

Two months later after my meeting with Mahmoud, I met a coworker of his who informed me that Mahmoud got married to a teacher of the same religion as him and from same village. This teacher was in the process of divorcing her husband, a railroad manager from another railroad station. After her divorce was finally issued, Mahmoud and this young lady got married.

In my next visit to his village, I visited Mahmoud at his office to wish him the very best in his new marriage. He surprised me that he was not so happy with his decision not to marry Rachel. He invited me to his house to meet his new wife. He seemed that he really wanted to talk to me. I was happy to see Mahmoud looking so happy with his recent marriage. He appeared to be happy and his face was shining.

When we sat down, he offered me coffee and talked about his new life in great detail. After dinner he took me to the station to catch my next train home. While we were waiting for my train, we suddenly saw Rachel coming off the train that had just arrived. I noticed that his face showed severe concern when he saw her. He invited her to come and sit down with us until my train arrived. She was a beautiful girl with black eyes and a slim figure. After the typical exchange of formalities she expressed real concerns about her future. She asked him why he did not come to the meeting they had agreed last Thursday.

I felt very sorry for this teenage girl. She was visibly deeply in love with him and she could not accept that he was now a married man seemingly in love with another woman. I also was upset with my friend's behavior. He never invited me to his wedding either. My words upset her even more and sad feelings clearly showed on her face and in her eyes.

The silence that followed in this small railroad waiting room clearly showed Rachel's misery and unhappiness towards her former lover. She could not forgive him for his decision to marry a different girl. She was willing to give up everything for him, even to change her religion in order to be accepted.

Rachel cried and told us how miserable she was. She said that she would never love another man; but life is unpredictable. It was possible that Rachel would meet another man of the same religion probably from the same village and from a good family. I never thought that her disappointment was going to stay deep in her sensitive young heart.

A few days after our meeting at the railroad station, during the middle of the night, a shadow was seen walking towards the banks of the Nile. It was September and the river was full, almost touching the bridge above. The shadow was Rachel, who had made a tragic decision to end her life. A couple of people crossing the bridge who saw Rachel walking towards its edge suspected her intentions to jump in the river. They tried to stop her but it was too late. Rachel's body was carried by the rushing water of the river until it disappeared. The next day, fishermen discovered her body floating in the Nile.

ΠΡΩΤΟΤΥΠΑ ΔΙΗΓΗΜΑΤΑ

ΓΙΑ ΤΗΝ ΑΓΑΠΗ ΤΟΥ ΜΑΧΜΟΥΤ

ΑΠΟ ΤΗ ΖΩΗ ΤΩΝ ΦΕΛΛΑΧΩΝ

Σ' ἕνα ἀπ' τὰ τακτικά μου ταξείδια, εἶχα γνωρίσει τὸν ὑποσταθμάρχη τοῦ σιδηροδρομικοῦ σταθμοῦ Μ. Ὁ Μαχμοὺτ—ἔτσι τὸν λέγαν—ἦταν ἕνας νέος εἴκοσι πέντε περίπου χρονῶν, μὲ γαλανὰ μάτια, μορφὴ πολὺ συμπαθητικὴ, κ' ἐρωτοπαθὴς ὅσο φαντασθῆτε. Ὅταν τὸν γνώρισα ἦταν ἐρωτευμένος μὲ δύο Ἑβραιοπούλες — τὴν Ρασὲλ καὶ τὴν Ρόζα, ἡ πρώτη μιὰ ῥαφτοπούλα, ἡ δεύτερη δαντέλα σ' ἕνα μεγάλο κατάστημα νεωτερισμῶν.

Μὲ τὶς συχνὲς ἐπισκέψεις καὶ τῶν δύο στὸ μικρὸ διαμέρισμα τοῦ σταθμοῦ, εἶχεν ἀποκτήσει — καὶ δίκαια — τὴν φήμη Δὸν Ζουάν.

Ξενυχτοῦσε κι' ὅλας, καὶ μὲ τὰ ξενύχτια του αὐτὰ ἄρχισε νὰ παραμελῇ καὶ τὴν δουλειά του. Ἕνα πρωΐ ἔφθασα μὲ τὸ πρῶτο τραῖνο. Μιὰ ἀσυνήθιστη κίνησι στὸν μικρὸ αὐτὸ ἐξοχικὸ σταθμό, καὶ ἡ ἀργοπορία γιὰ τὴν ἀναχώρησι τοῦ τραίνου, μ' ἔκαμαν νὰ καταλάβω πὼς κάτι συνέβαινε.

Κατέβηκα, βρῆκα τὸν Μαχμοὺτ, κ' ἔμαθα πὼς ἔπειτα ἀπὸ ξενύχτι δυὸ μερῶν, παράλαβε νυκτερινὴ ὑπηρεσία, κι' ἄϋπνος κ' ἐξηντλημένος καθὼς ἦταν, δὲν ἄργησε νὰ κοιμηθῇ.

Στὶς τέσσαρες τὸ πρωΐ, ἕνα φορτηγὸ τραῖνο, μπαίνοντας ἀντιθέτως στὸ σταθμό, ποὺ ὁ Μαχμοὺτ ἦταν κι' ὁ κλειδοῦχος, ὅταν ἦτο σὲ νυχτερινὴ ὑπηρεσία, δὲν ἄλλαξε γραμμὴ, κ' ἔτσι τὸ τραῖνο ἐκτροχιάσθηκε, κ' ἔφραξε τὸν δρόμο τῆς ἐπιβατικοῦ ποὺ ταξείδευα, δίχως εὐτυχῶς νὰ ὑπάρξουν ἀνθρώπινα θύματα. Μὲ τὰ μέσα ὅμως ποὺ διέθετε, κατώρθωσε νὰ ἀπαλλαγῇ τῆς εὐθύνης, μὲ πρόστιμο μόνον δεκαπέντε ἡμερῶν ἀπὸ τὸν μισθό του.

Εἶχε περάσει πειὰ ἀρκετὸς καιρὸς ἀπὸ τότε, ὅπου μιὰ μέρα λαμβάνω ἕνα γράμμα του. Μοὖγραφε πὼς τὸ ἐρχόμενο Σάββατο θὰ μὲ περίμενε σπίτ'

τος, γιὰ νὰ μοῦ πῇ κάτι τὸ σοβαρὸ ποὺ τοῦ συμβαίνει. Ὅταν πῆγα, περίεργος γιὰ νὰ μάθω, τὸν βρῆκα μελαγχολικὸ κι' ἀνυπόμονο νὰ μὲ περιμένῃ.

— Ξεύρεις πῶς ἀγαπῶ τὴν Ρασέλ ! ! !

— Καὶ τὴν Ρόζα — αὐτὴν δὲν τὴν ἀγαπᾷς πειά ;

— Μὰ φίλε μου, ἐδῶ πρόκειται γιὰ γάμο. Θὰ παντρευθῶ τὴν Ρασέλ.

Μ' ἔπιασαν ἄθελα τὰ γέλοια.

— Σοῦ μιλῶ σοβαρά.

— Μὰ δὲν μπ.. ' νὰ καταλάβω, Μαχμοὺτ, πῶς θὰ παντρευθῆς μιὰ ἀλλόθρησκή σου, καὶ, τὸ κυριώτερο, δάχως τὴν ἄδεια τοῦ πατέρα σου.

— Ὅσο γιὰ τὴν Ρασέλ, θ' ἀσπασθῇ τὴν θρησκεία μου, καὶ γιὰ τὸν πατέρα μου εἶμαι βέβαιος πὼς θὰ μὲ συγχωρήσῃ γιὰ τὸν γάμο μου αὐτό, γιατί μ' ἀγαπᾷ ἐξαιρετικά.

— Δὲν βρίσκω διόλου λογικὰ τὰ ἐπιχειρήματά σου γιὰ τὸν γάμο αὐτό, Μαχμούτ.

— Ἀδιάφορῶ, ἀγαπητέ μου γιὰ ὅ..., καὶ σοῦ ἐπαναλαμβάνω τὴν ἀπόφασι ποὺ ἔχω πάρει, νὰ παντρευθῶ τὴν Ρασέλ.....

Εἶνε ἐρωτευμένος στὰ καλὰ ὁ φίλος μου, σκέφθηκα. Ποθοῦσε τὴν Ρασέλ. Κι' ὁ πόθος του αὐτὸς τὸν ἔσπρωχνε στὴν τρελλή του ἀπόφασι — ποὺ γι' αὐτὸν ἦταν ὁ γάμος. Ἤξευρε πῶς ἡ Ρασὲλ τὸν ἀγαποῦσε. Τὴν τρελλή λοιπὸν ἀγάπη μιᾶς κόρης δεκάξη χρονῶν θὰ χρησίμευε γιὰ ν' ἀποσπάσῃ μιὰ φτωχὴ κόρη — ἀπὸ ἕνα φτωχὸ πατρικὸ σπίτι.

* * * * *

Δυὸ μῆνες εἶχα νὰ ἰδῶ τὸν Μαχμοὺτ ἀπ' τὴν τελευταία μας συνάντησι. Ἕνας συνάδελφός του, ποὺ μὲ συνήντησε τυχαίως, μοῦ εἶπε πῶς ὁ φίλος μου παντρεύθηκε μὲ μιὰ ὁμόθρησκό του δασκάλα καὶ νὰ πῶς. Ἡ δασκάλα αὐτὴ

ἦταν στὰ χωρίσματα μὲ τὸν ἄνδρα της
— σταθμάρχη ἑνὸς ἄλλου μικροῦ προα-
στείου τῆς πρωτευούσης. Ὁ Μαχμούτ
λοιπὸν ἀνέλαβε νὰ συμβιβάσῃ τ' ἀνδρό-
γυνο, καὶ στὰς διαπραγματεύσεις των
ἐπάνω, ἀγαπηθήκανε, χώρισεν ὁριστι-
κὰ ἀπ' τὸν πρῶτον της ἄνδρα καὶ παντρεύθηκε τὸν Μαχμούτ.

Ἀπεφάσισα πεὰ νὰ πάγω πρὸς συ-
νάντησί του, καὶ νὰ τὸν εὐχηθῶ. Μὲ
δέχθηκε μὲ τὴν συνειθισμένη του κα-
λωσύνη. Καὶ μιὰ χαρὰ ἀκτινοβολοῦσε
στὸ συμπαθητικὸ πρόσωπό του. Ἦταν
ἡ χαρὰ τοῦ νεονύμφου.

Ἄρχισε νὰ μοῦ διηγῆται γιὰ τὸν
ἀπρόσοπο γάμο του, ὅταν ξαφνικὰ εἴ-
δαμε τὴν Ραοὲλ, νὰ κατεβαίνῃ ἀπὸ τὸ
μόλις ἀφιχθὲν τραῖνο.

Μιὰ ταραχὴ παρατήρησα στὸ πρόσωπό του, κι' αὐτὸ μ' ἔπεισε πὼς ἡ μικροῦλα δὲν γνώριζε τοὺς γάμους του.

Ἡ Ραοὲλ, μιὰ μικροῦλα δεκάξη τὸ
πολὺ χρονῶν, κοντούλα, μὲ κουκλίστι-
κο προσωπάκι, μεγάλα μαῦρα μάτια,
ἦλθε καὶ κάθισε μαζύ μας, μέσα στὸ
μικρὸ διαμέρισμα τοῦ σταθμοῦ, μ' ὁλο-
φάνερη τὴν ἀγωνία τῆς προαισθήσεως
στὸ συμπαθητικό της προσωπάκι.

Ἔπειτα ἀπὸ τὰ τυπικὰ φιλοφρονή-
ματα τοῦ φίλου μου, τοῦ παραπονεῖτο
πῶς, ἀφοῦ τῆς ἔδωσε συνέντευξι τὴν
Πέμπτη τὸ βράδυ, ἐκεῖνος δὲν πῆγε.
Ποῦ νὰ φανταστῇ ἡ καὶμένη πὼς, τὴν
ἡμέραν ἐκείνη, μιὰ ἄλλη εἶχε κυριεύ-
σει τὴν ἄστατη καρδιά του, καὶ ὅτι τὴν
ὥρα ἀκριβῶς αὐτή, παντρεμμένος πιά,
κι' εὐτυχισμένος στὴν ἀγκαλιὰ τῆς νό-
μιμης γυναίκας του, ὑπόσχετο μὲ ὅρ-
κους αἰώνια ἀγάπη, ὅπως λίγες μέρες
πρὶν, τὰ ἴδια λόγια ἀγάπης ὑπόσχετο
καὶ σ' αὐτὴν τὴν πτωχὴ κι' ὀρφανευμέ-
νη πιὰ καρδιά της.

Αἰσθανόμενος τὴν δύσκολη θέσι του,
καὶ γιὰ νὰ δώσω ἕνα τέλος, τῆς εἶπα
ὅτι κι' ἐγὼ ἔχω παράπονα μὲ τὸν Μαχμούτ, γιατί παντρεύθηκε τὴν Πέμπτη,
καὶ ὅμως δὲν μ' ἐκάλεσε στοὺς γάμους
του.

Τὰ λόγια μου αὐτὰ τὴν ἐτάραξαν, τὸ
μικρὸ προσωπάκι της χλώμιασε, ἐνῶ
ἀπὸ τὰ ὁλόμαυρα μάτια της, ἄρχισαν
νὰ λάμπουν, σὰν ἀντανάκλασις μαργα-
ριτῶν, τὰ δάκρυα.

Στὴ σιωπὴ ποὺ ἀπλώθηκε μέσ' στὸ
μικρὸ διαμέρισμα τοῦ σταθμοῦ, ἄκου-
σα τ' ἀναφυλλητὰ τῆς μικρῆς, σὰν ἕνα
παράπονο γιὰ τὴν ἀπιστία τοῦ ἀγαπη-
μένου της, ποὺ γιὰ τὴν ἀγάπη του, καὶ
τὴν θρησκεία της θ' ἀρνιότανε.

Πτωχὴ Ραοὲλ, σὰν ποιήτη που ἀ-
γάπη, ἦταν φτιαχτῆ τὰ αἰσθανθῆς τὴν
τὰ μεγάλη ἀπογοήτευσι τῆς ζωῆς σου.
Θὰ ὑποφέρῃς καὶ σὰν ὅπως ὅλοι σὰν
ἀρχή, θὰ κλάψῃς, θὰ πονέσῃς, ἕνας
ἄλλος ὅμως θὰ βρεθῆ — ὁμοιθρησκός
σου—ποῦ θὰ σ' ἀγαπήσῃ στ' ἀλήθεια.
Κι' ὅταν, ἀνθοστολισμένη κι' ὄμορφη
νυφούλα θὰ γέρνῃς στὴν ἀγκαλιά του,
— θὰ ξεχάσῃς τὸν πόνο σου. Ἔπειτα
εἶσαι τόσον μικροῦλα ἀκόμη ! ! Αὐτὰ
τὰ παρήγορα λόγια τῆς ἔλεγα, γνω-
ρῶντας μαζύ της ἀπ' τὸ προάστειο στὴν
πόλι μέσα στὸ τραῖνο...Ποῦ νὰ φαντα-
σθῶ ὅμως πὼς ἡ ἀπογοήτευσις θὰ ἔ-
μενε βαθειὰ ριζωμένη μέσ' τὴν εὐαί-
σθητη καρδούλα της.

Μέσ' τὸ σκοτάδι τῆς νύχτας, μιὰ
σκιὰ προχωρεῖ πρὸς τὴν ὄχθη. Εἶνε
Σεπτέμβριος μήνας, ποὺ ὁ Νεῖλος,
φουσκωμένος ὅπως ἦτο, εἶχε φθάσει
τὰ τόξα τῆς μεγάλης γέφυρας. Τὰ βα-
ρειὰ καὶ θολὰ νερά του, ἀθόρυβα κυ-
λοῦνε μέσ' τὴν κατάμαυρη νύκτα.

Ἡ Ραοὲλ αὐτὴ ἦταν ἡ
σκιά—εἶχε πάρει τὴ μεγάλη καὶ τραγι-
κή της ἀπόφασι. Ἡ ἀπόγνωσίς της τὴν
ἔσπρωχνε πρὸς τὴν αὐτοκτονία.

Ὅταν μερικοὶ διαβάται ἀντελήφθη-
καν τὴν πρόθεσί της — ἦταν πλέον ἀρ-
γά. Τὸ ὁρμητικὸ ρεῦμα τοῦ μεγάλου
ποταμοῦ, εἶχε σκεπάσει μὲ λαχτάρα τὸ
νεανικὸ της κορμί.

Μόνον τὴν ἄλλη μέρα κατὰ τὸ δείλι
ἕτι ψαράδες βρῆκαν τὸ πτῶμα της,
ὃ ἐπέπλεε.

NIKOΣ ΘΕΟΤΟΚΑΤΟΣ

ΘΛΟΥΣΙΟΝ ΚΛΛΟΙΤΖ - Ἐνοικιάζεται

14

Takis Theotocatos:
My Story

From Phoenix, Arizona

M y father, Nicos Theotocatos, owned a farm outside Alexandria, Egypt until his death in 1954. After his death, I had to quit my Greek high school and with my mother, Stella, we managed the farm. After struggling for four years to hold onto the land, we finally had to give it up and allow the government of Gamal Abdel Nasser, the President of Egypt, to nationalize it. By the late 1950s, most of private land in Egypt was nationalized, including ours.

After we lost the farm, my mother and I moved to Alexandria where I got a job with the Greek newspaper *Tachydromos*. Looking at the horrible future ahead of me, I decided to leave Egypt and join my brother George who lived in New York at the time.

When I decided to leave Egypt, I visited the Greek Embassy to get an exit visa and I was shocked to find out that the Egyptian government treated me as an Egyptian citizen. I was told that in order to get an exit visit, I had to serve in the Egyptian Military Service in Cairo for three years! Only then would the Egyptian authorities allow me to change my nationality to that of a Greek citizen. After my research on this subject, I found out that my father had dropped his Greek citizenship to become an Egyptian citizen a few years before he died. We are not sure why he did that, which was very unusual for Greeks and other Europeans who lived in the country at that time.

The prospects of a Greek boy serving in the Egyptian military and returning home after completing his service were not very good. We heard firsthand the horror stories from the few who survived and came home. A friend of mine was aware of all the problems I had trying to leave Egypt. He suggested that I should contact an Egyptian general that his family knew very well. He said that this general could handle my case successfully if I followed his advice and signed up with the Egyptian Army for three years but, in reality, I would only spend three days in the barracks in Cairo. On the fourth day, I would leave the barracks with a certificate stating that I had met my Egyptian military obligations. He would take care of all the details for this very risky deal. The cost for this secret operation was paying this general secretly the equivalent of $30,000! This amount was all the savings we had in our bank.

I was so desperate to leave Egypt that I accepted this deal and made plans to go to Cairo sometime in the next several months, as soon as I received a call from the Egyptian general. I was so scared that this whole affair would blow up on my face and I would end up in the Egyptian Army for three years. Also, I was taking a big risk that I would probably never make it out of the military alive! But I had no choice; I accepted the general's offer and started paying him monthly installments towards our agreement of $30,000.

While all this trauma and stress was happening in my life for several years, I met Frank K. in a bar in Alexandria in 1961. (Because of the sensitivity of some of the subjects discussed here I have decided not to disclose Frank's identity.) At the time, Frank was a Harvard student traveling all over Europe and Egypt. His family was well connected with the Boston elites, including the Kennedys. Frank and I spent a couple of weeks at the local bar getting to know each other. I liked him very much as a new friend, confessing to him my entire situation about the Egyptian general getting me a military service certificate. He told me to give this general a chance to help me, but if anything concerning this deal failed, I should immediately contact a person he knew very well in London. This person was very well connected in the United States and the Middle East. If the plan with the general did not work out, he would find another way to get me out of Egypt and seek political asylum in the United States.

Luckily for me, the Egyptian Army plan worked out precisely. I got my Greek passport and left Egypt for Greece with my mother. I spent a few months in Greece while my brother George was making plans to enroll me at the Rhodes Preparatory School in Manhattan to complete my secondary education, which was interrupted after my father's death. I was finally admitted at Rhodes and obtained a student visa to come to the United States to study.

I arrived in New York in 1962 at the age of twenty-four—free at last and ready to work hard and make a new life for myself. A couple of years later, I completed all academic requirements and graduated from Rhodes School in 1964.

Immediately after graduation from Rhodes, I applied and was accepted at New York University's Washington Square Campus in New York. A few months later, as I went to the cafeteria for lunch, whom do I see there? Frank K. He had just graduated from Harvard University and had come to NYU to get his law degree. We stayed in close touch and became really good friends. One day during my senior year, he asked me about my plans after graduation.

"Well," I said, "with my lousy grade average [going to school full time, including summers, and working as a waiter in the evenings did not leave me much free time for studying], I would be very lucky if a company would hire me for a one-year training program. At the end of this program, I would have to go back to Greece."

Frank looked at me with a big smile and said, "Let's meet next week to discuss your options. I might have something for you."

A week later, we met for lunch and he asked me to call Bobby Kennedy's campaign manager (yes, JFK's brother) and give him my name. The next day, I did exactly what Frank suggested and called the manager in Robert Kennedy's New York office. After the initial introductions, the manager offered me a job to be the driver for the Kennedy office in New York. I of course accepted the job. It was hard work but also a lot of fun. I was treated very well. The fact that I was a close friend of Frank's certainly helped.

I graduated from NYU in 1968 and immediately met with Frank to ask his advice on how to proceed with getting a regular job.

"Apply for U.S. citizenship and don't worry about it," he advised.

"Frank, are you nuts? My application will end up in the wastebasket in ten seconds after the INS [Immigration and Naturalization] people read it."

"Just do it!" was his strong reply.

I followed Frank's instructions and three months later, I received a registered letter from INS welcoming me to the USA with a green card included in the envelope. This meant that I was now a permanent resident of the States and had all the rights of an American citizen, except the right to vote. Five years later, I took the oath and became an American citizen. Neither Frank nor the Kennedy's office manager ever shared how this miracle happened but I was grateful for it.

In February 1968, Paula (my girlfriend at the time) and I both applied for a job with IBM and they hired us on the spot (another miracle). The company assigned us to the same IBM branch office on Wall Street. Three years later, Paula and I got married.

Once in a while, I reminisce about my past and I still can't believe all the miracles that happened that led me to the same IBM branch office where my best friend and wife, Panayota (Paula) Theotocatos, and I started our careers. My incredible story is a reminder that these things only happen in America. You can now see what an incredible role Frank K. has played in my life, both in Egypt and in the U.S.

Paula and I worked for IBM for 25 years then retired to Naples, Florida. Naples is one of the most beautiful cities in the United States. Unfortunately, the heat, humidity and insects during the summer months made our lives unbearable. So in 2002, we finally gave up and selected Phoenix, Arizona as our retirement place. We currently live in Anthem Arizona and are very happy with our retirement choice.

15

Yiannis Barbas:
My Story

From Columbus, Ohio

I have asked my two living cousins to share their stories below. The first cousin, Yiannis Barbas, is the only child of my uncle George, the older brother of my mother. He is married to Chrysoula. They live in Columbus, Ohio and have one daughter, Patricia, who is married to Jeff Phillips, and have two grandchilden, Emmanuel and Lewis. Here is his story.

My Uncle George, cousin Yiannis, his mother Patra
and me in Thessaloniki in 1968.

I am known to my friends as Yannis, the Greek version of John. To my parents and family, I was always Yannaki, or Little John, as well as Little Why, because everything in life was a "why" for me since the time I could talk—not because of questioning authority, but simple curiosity.

My father George and mother Patra were born in Cairo and Kafr El Zayat, respectively, and were married in 1946. George, a chemical engineer, studied at the University of Strasburg in France. After World War II, both my parents immigrated to Addis Ababa, Ethiopia, where my father worked as a chemist at a soap producing company. It was with this capacity that he met Emperor Haile Selassie.

Eight years later, they returned to Egypt. My father secured a job as a chemist at one of the biggest chemical factories in Kaftr El Zayat, owned by another Greek, Dimitirs Zerbinis. In that capacity, my father became a leading authority in chlorine production.

I was born in Alexandria in 1954 and grew up in Kaft El Zayat until I finished second grade. At that time, the Greek school in our little town had deteriorated and my parents sent me to Alexandria to live with my Aunt Stella and Cousin Takis. Once there, I attended the Kokinarios Greek School.

I recall vividly one day in Spring 1962, while I was at home in Kafr El Zayat, a couple of well-suited Egyptian gentlemen came to visit us. I had no idea who they were or the purpose of their visit, but I do remember that the atmosphere at home became very tense afterwards.

Next thing I knew, in June 1962, we had packed our household and boarded a steamship at Suez heading for Greece, where we started a new life. My father had accepted a position as a technical director and chemist at a new factory in Salonika, in northern Greece. While moving into our new house, Cousin Takis, on his way out of Egypt to the United States, arrived to help us with the move; a few days later he was boarding the S/S Atlantic for America.

In Salonika, I attended school through the eleventh grade. Then my father's factory ceased operations and my father took an early retirement, moving to Athens to be near relatives on my mother's side.

Growing up, I started to ask my parents more about our past in Egypt and the reasons we left. It was then that I learned about those Egyptian gentlemen who had visited us at home when I was just seven years old. It was right after Nasser had nationalized all foreign industries and Europeans were leaving en mass. Those visitors were government officials who knew of my father's reputation as a chlorine production authority and were trying to recruit him to join in some secret chemical project. He immediately suspected that the proposition had the potential to transition to chemical weapons production. That, in conjunction with the ordeal that Cousin Takis had just experienced with the looming military service, was the catalyst for our immediate and hasty departure for Greece.

Since I was a toddler, my interests were always focused on technical matters and my father, being an engineer, made sure he kept fueling that interest. However, at the age of nine, aeronautics entered my life through plain observation that soon evolved into a passion. My life was consumed by airplanes and flying. Everything I read and researched was around aviation.

Unfortunately, this field was extremely closed in Greece of those years. I attempted to enroll in the Hellenic Air Force Academy, but the nine available slots the year of my high school graduation went to sons and nephews of Greek generals and government officials. The only other available option was to try entering Onassis' Olympic Airways, which up until then would recruit young men and send them to England for pilot training. Unfortunately, my timing was off; the untimely death of Onassis' son Alexander, and subsequent sale of the airline to the government, led to the cancellation of the program.

It became apparent that if I were to pursue my dreams, I would have to go abroad for studies. My father supported me but our finances were limited. I enrolled in a technical school in Athens to study aviation maintenance until a plan could be worked out. While studying, I would spend endless hours between the Athens airport and a technical library in our community where a young, beautiful librarian had started working. Little did I know that this cute, blue-eyed librarian, Chryssoula, would become my wife after five-and-a-half years.

After graduation, I entered the Hellenic Air Force for my mandatory military service, having formulated a plan that after discharge I would come to America to complete my studies. In the meantime, I started contacting schools and saving money to at least start the journey.

In June 1977, immediately after my separation from the Air Force, Chryssoula and I got married and five days later we were deplaning at JFK Airport in New York, into the unknown to start a new and married life.

To understand the struggles we had in starting our new life, one must understand the economic climate of Greece at that time. The small funds my father had managed to save for my studies proved impossible to extract from Greece. The Bank of Greece, which at that time had to approve any export of student funds, refused to allow me to take the money, because in their opinion the field of aeronautics was closed in Greece. They would not even consider the idea that I could seek employment anywhere else but Greece. In their reasoning, they would be allowing currency to flow out of the country with no prospect of ever recovering it from me.

We were fortunate that a distant relative worked for a commercial bank and helped us transfer the mere $4,000 to a bank in New Jersey through a maritime shipping account—a perfectly legal loophole! I handed off the cash, hoping I would see the money in few weeks in New Jersey. I did, but those funds were not adequate to complete my studies. The INS would have never granted us visas to enter the country not even as student, unless we had a sponsor.

It was at this point where life came full circle. Cousin Takis, years before us, had experienced even harder struggles trying to get out of Egypt and was helped by a good friend. He now came through for us. As soon as our plan was formulated, Takis became our mentor, guide and ultimate supporter. He was already established at IBM and provided all the guidance we needed to come to the U.S. as newlyweds to start our life and my dream of becoming an aviator. He signed an affidavit with

INS that he would support us if need be and would be responsible for us.

On July 7, 1977, I started studies at one of the best flight schools in the country. When my limited funds were exhausted, Takis cosigned a student loan and I was able to complete my studies, paying the loan back in record time. My passion for flying manifested through outstanding performance in school, to the point that upon graduation I was the first student of the school to be offered a position as an instructor in the school, helping me and my wife obtain green cards. My wife was hired by the president of the school as a nanny, and thus our life in America had started. Five years later, in 1984, we both became U.S. citizens a year after our daughter Patricia was born.

My career moved in a very predictable path. I became an airline pilot with a major U.S. carrier, moved up the ranks and having realized my childhood dream, made it an objective to someday help educate and train people in aviation, giving what I had longed for as a youngster. I was once told that someday I would teach at a university. I have come full circle now, having been offered a position to teach aviation courses at The Ohio State University.

I mentioned earlier how I met the woman that would become my wife by studying in a library. It is interesting to note that through my passion for aeronautics I not only enjoyed a magnificent and fulfilling career, but also got together with the one human being who would be a catalyst in my advancements.

Since 1977, Chryssoula has stood by me through the most difficult academic years, furloughs and successes. In 1983, she gave birth to our wonderful daughter, Patricia, who in 2008 was married to Jeff Philips and together they gave us two adorable grandsons, Emmanuel (2014) and Lewis (2017). Another interesting aspect of our passion for education and expanding one's intellect was our insistence in our daughter getting a proper education. It is no surprise that she earned a graduate degree in English language and became a specialist of English literacy!

As a family, we kept alive our Greek customs and traditions and we've embraced the American culture and way of life, managing to blend the best of both cultures. It was interesting when, upon announcing Patricia's engagement, friends asked if she was to marry a Greek boy. My joke has always been that she was marrying a man named Philips, a name that has the Greek root "Philipos" and therefore, yes, she was marrying someone with Greek roots. In reality, it made abso-

Yiannis, Chrysoula, Emmanuel and Lewis
in Pittsburgh in 2018.

lutely no difference to us what Jeff's background was. The only thing that mattered and continues to matter is that he is a good man, loves and cares for his family, and most importantly, respects us.

And life goes on, always remember those who have helped you, and continue to do the same for those who follow. At this point, I believe it is of interest to interject a translated letter of a great uncle of mine that may help you understand the sagas of my ancestors scattered all ove the world. My paternal relatives trace part of their roots to what was known until the early 1900s as Asia Minor, today's Turkey—the northern shores of Turkey, by the Black Sea, and the shores by the Aegean Sea, what remnants of ancient Greek colonies collectively called Asia Minor. In 1922, after a bloody and unsuccessful campaign of the Greek Army to penetrate deep into Turkey and reclaim those old Greek towns, the Turks launched a purging counter-campaign driving out the Greek population.

The last remaining members of my family lived in the area of Sinope and Samsun, on the shores of Black Sea. In fact, my paternal grandfather and his siblings were born in Sinope, birthplace of the great ancient philosopher Diogenes of Sinope, founder of the School of Cynics.

My grandfather John, with his mother, sisters and brothers, had left Sinope for Egypt before World War I. His brother Dimitri stayed behind in Samsun, which at that time the Greeks called Amisos, or Samisos.

To put the letter in context, the Turks had rounded up all the Greek population and were driving them to places unknown, a treacherous journey on foot, which for most ended in death. Upon arrival at Gerze (Kerze in Greek), Great-Uncle Dimitri wrote a letter to his mother, sisters and brothers. He handed this letter to a British soldier heading to Istanbul and asked him mail it. What a hopeless attempt that miraculously materialized! I recommend searching Google Earth for these locales so as to gain a better perspective.

Kerze, 17 March 1919

My respected mother and dearest sisters and brothers,
You know what happened to us during the course of World War [ed. WWI]. As you know I stayed in Amisos [ed. Samsun], but as soon as the general conscription was ordered, I sent my family to Kerze [ed. Gerze] and I stayed here to work at a store with my boss, who continued to pay me since I was excluded of any military service. However, because everyone else was conscripted and business had almost died,

they cut my salary by half and I was forced to leave Amisos and come here around the end of December 1914. Since the high school was closed due to lack of teacher, I resumed my old profession as teacher for a meager salary, even though I had decided to never teach again; however, God's wish is not the same as that of men.

During the second year of the war, as soon as final exams were completed on 24 June 1916, it was ordered that we would be unjustly and unfairly be expelled from the town. The very next dawn, two policemen started banging on doors, directing all males to report to the courthouse where we were held for 30 hours. Two hours after our arrest, they forced all crying women to gather their children and most essential necessities, and board a horse-drawn carriage that took them in the fields, out of town. There they spent the entire night in the fields, waiting for their husbands to arrive the following day.

Indeed, the following day we were reunited with our families under military escort and the signal was given to begin a march to the unknown. With tears in our eyes we bid farewell to our beloved homeland and friends, not knowing where they were taking us or whether we would have the same fate as the Armenians [ed. the Armenian population was massacred]. After passing several small towns, the surviving 30 families arrived in Kerze, where we were distributed to various villages within 12 hours walk from here.

One cannot even begin to imagine the suffering we endured and the tears we shed, for three days and nights, but after realizing we were no longer in danger for our lives, we slowly adapted to the monotonous life. We spent two and a half months in peace. However, realizing that winter was approaching and without any money and work, we knew we would suffer and most likely die of starvation and cold, so we moved to Saframboli, 12 hours from Kerze, and settled there. I cannot describe the suffering we endured; many perished in those foreign lands. However, I am happy that we survived, and we were fortunate to return to our homes. Since then, I have been out of work, and we have no furniture, clothes, nor shoes, because we were forced – like most – to sell everything just to be able to buy bread. Thank God for saving us and keeping us healthy, and enabling us to return home.

For quite some time I've been meaning to write to you and let you know that your lost brother exists, but there was no mail service. Today, I learned that in Istanbul and Alexandria there are British Posts and I decided to write to you and send this letter with a passenger to Istanbul praying that God will deliver it to your hands. I was hopping until now to receive a letter from you, but I was not that fortunate. I wonder if I will ever receive a letter from you, to see your signatures, so that I may kiss them and wet them with tears of joy and relief. Will I ever learn that our mother is still alive and all are healthy?

I would like to let you know that our daughter Marika got married to Kyriakos Harpidis. After his first wife died, he asked for Marika's hand and they were married nine months ago, and God willing she will become mother in three months. Our son-in- law, whom I believe you know, is well to do, one of the largest merchants, but has many children. What can I say? This was her destiny and what the circumstances dictated.

Below is a copy of Dimitrios' original letter in Greek sent from Kerje, Asia Minor, dated March 17, 1919. Note the faded round stamp on the top left of the date.This is the British Postal Service's censorship stamp.

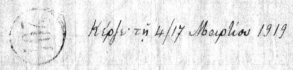

Κέρκ(υρα) τῇ 4/17 Μαρτίου 1919

Σεβαστή μοι μῆτερ καί φροφημοι
ἀδελφοί καί ἀδελφαί

Σᾶς εἶναι γνωστά ὅτι ὑπέστημεν κατά τό διαστημα τοῦ ὀχεδρίου σαψνοσμιου πολέμου ἐν Ἀμισσῷ δια-
μένων, ὡς γνωρίζετε, ἐδῶ ὡς ὑπηρχθη ἡ γενική ἐκ-
στρατευσις, τήν μέν ἀπεχχμαι μου ἔδηχεν ἐνταῦθα
ἐγώ δέ εἰσηχχαρμένος τον ὀχρμεῖα, καί ὑπρεπεαῦμα
νά εἶμαι ἐν τῷ καλεστημεσι μόνος μετά τῶν φροϋστα-
μένων μου, ὀηρωσεύντων ἐκρέσως τό ὀχρεκεσλικόν ἀντι-
σημηκεσι των· ἀλλ' ἐπειδή πεῖνδε οἱ ὑπαίγχησον ἐϊρελο-
ληχμένωσεν καί ἡ γιγγοβοσία ἠμαλλώδη, ἔπαυσεν τό ἤ-
μισυ τοῦ μισθοῦ μου, οὕτε δί ἐμή ἐπανοσωσούμενος ἀναγ-
καιόσθην ν' ἀναχαιρησίων τήν Ἀμισσόν ἰηδιω δέ ἐνταῦθα
μέσον Πάτρας–Ἀλικόσαμι φερί τά ἔξη Σεπτεμβρίου 1914,
ὑμοδῶ δι' ὅσσς τήν σχεσιν δι'ἔχμιη διδεοσιόχου, ἀνέλα-
βον καί φάζμι τό διδεισιπαχκόν ἐφάζχυρα ἐπί ἐλληρ-
σλιεκδω μισθῶ, καίτοι, ὡς γνωρίζετε, ἔχον ἀπόφασιν νά μή

188

νάχεω σχέον τὸν διδάσκαλον, ἀλλ' ἄλλοι μὲν βοηθεῖ ἀνθρώπων, ἄλλοι δὲ διὰ τιμῆς. Τὸ δεύτερον ἔτος τοῦ σχέσιου μέχρι Σεπτεμβρίου ταῖς Πλειάσιν, τῇ 24 Ἰουνίου 1916, ἐισφεισόδευσις τῆς αἰδίου καὶ αἰδιμασχχίου ἐισχεσόσεως μας σχέ τὴν εὐχήν, δύο αἰδημόρεω προσδότε ἀσχιόνως ταῖς δύρ̄ μας σχοσεμέχρου καὶ ἀδήχου ὅμως τοὺς ἀνδρῶν εἰς τὸ δικαστήριον, ἵνα ἐμείναμεν ὑπὸ κράτησιν 30 ὅσας ὥρας· δύο ὥρας μετὰ τὴν σύγχησίν μας, ὁδηγοῦντες μίαν εἰρκτὴν, ὑσωχρ̄ .... σχεισόστεις γυναικῶν μας καὶ σχαραχαίδωσις ὅτι ταῖς .... καὶ .... ὅδηχαδίωσι δ' εἰς τοὺς ἀχροὺς μετὰ τῶν ἵππων τῶν καὶ εἰς τὸ δειπνηρον δεχεδοῦσαι τὴν νύκτα ἀνέμεναν τοὺς συζύγους των· ἐπὶ τέσοις τὴν ἐσχερινὴν ἐν συνοδίᾳ στρατιωτῶν ἀδηχάδημεν καὶ ἐχρῆτε ἐπὶ, δοδίντος δ' ἐπ' τοῦ συνθήχατος τῆς ἐναχωρήσεις μιας, Λαὶ δειπρύων ἐισχχωραδίσημεν τὴν σχρσοργὴν σαρτρίδα, μὴ γνωρίζοντες σοῦ ἀδηχούμεδα ἢ ἀν μᾶς ἀνέμενεν ἡ τύχη τῶν Ἀρμενίων· διεχδότε τὸ Πσϊανάλ, Γαῖς-μοσροῦ, Κιοδαμονῆ καὶ Γαλάτων, ἡχαλεῶν σχερὶ ταῖς 30 οἰκοχένεαι Κέρφρε διετμηάδημεν εἰς ταῖ 12 ὥρας ἀισάγοντα τῆς Γαλάτων χωρία αὐτῆς ἀπαὶ μία οἰκοχένεα εἰς ἔκαστον νεμηχεῖν· καὶ μόνον

189

ν' ἀναλογισθῇ τις τούς κόπους καί τούς ἱδρῶτας φρίκη τόν καταλαμβάνει· ἐπί 3 ἡμερονύκτια ἐδακρύσαμεν, ἀλλά κατόπιν πεισθέντες ὅτι οὐδένα διατρέχομεν κίνδυνον καί ἐξοικειωθέντες εἰς τήν μονότονον ἐκείνην ζωήν, 2½ μῆνας ἐζήσαμεν ἐν πλήρει ἡσυχίᾳ· σκεφθείς ὅμως ὅτι πλησιάζει ὁ χειμών καί ἄνευ χρημάτων καί ἐργασίας θά δυστυχήσωμεν καί θά κινδυνεύσωμεν νά ἀποθάνωμεν τῆς πείνης καί τοῦ ψύχους, μετετοπίσθημεν εἰς τήν 12 ὥρας ἐκ τοῦ χωρίου μου ἀπέχουσαν [illegible] καί ἀποκατεστάθην ἐκεῖ· ὅσα ὑπεφέραμεν διά τήν συντήρησίν μας δέν περιγράφονται, ἐν τούτοις ἂν καί πολλοί εἶπαν τά κακά εἰς τάς ξένας χώρας, εἴμεθα εὐτυχεῖς· διότι ἠξιώθημεν νά ἐπανέλθωμεν εἰς τάς ἑστίας μας· εὑρίσκομαι εἰσέτι ἄνευ ἐργασίας καί δέν μας ἔμειναν οὔτε ἔπιπλα οὔτε ἐνδύματα, διότι κδώ καί πάντες οἱ ἄλλοι, ἠναγκάσθημεν νά ἐκποιήσωμεν αὐτά καί νά προμηθευώμεθα τόν ἐπιούσιον ἄρτον· δόξα τῷ θεῷ τῷ διαφυλάξαντι ἡμᾶς ὑγιεῖς καί ἀξιώσαντι νά ἐπανέλθωμεν.

Ἀπό πολλοῦ ἐπεθύμουν νά σοί γράψω καί δηλώσω ὅτι ὁ ἀπολωλώς ἀδελφός σου εὑρέθη, ἀλλά δέν ὑπάρχει συγκοι-

νεντία ταχυδρομική· σήμερον δὲ ἔμαθον ὅτι ἐν Καΐρῳ
ᾧ εἰς Ἀλεξάνδρειαν ὑπάρχει Ἀγγλικὸν ταχυδρομεῖον, σᾶς
παρακαλῶ νὰ σᾶς γράψω καὶ μὴ ἐκβάλλων τινὰ καὶ ὀλίγην
τὴν σταυροῦσάν μου εἰς Κάϊρον· εὔχομαι ὁ Θεὸς νὰ τὴν
ὀλίγην τῶν χειρῶν σας. Ἤγγου μέχρι σήμερον νὰ μ... τὸ
κοινὸν γράμμα σας, ἀλλὰ δὲν τὸ ἠξεύδεω· εἴπαμε διὰ ἀ-
ξιωθῶ νὰ λάβω τὰ γραμμάτια σας, νὰ ἴδω μίαν ὑπογρα-
φήν σας, διὰ νὰ ... αὐτοκατόθε καὶ βρέξε μὲ δάκρυα χα-
ρᾶς καὶ ἀγαλλιάσεως· δὲν ἐξεύδει νὰ μάθω ὅτι ἡ μή-
τηρ μας ζῇ καὶ σῶσθε ὑγιαίνει;

    Ἔστε ὥρα γνώσει σας ὅτι τὴν Μαρίναν μας τὴν ὑπαν-
δρεύσαμεν ὁ Κυριακὸς Χαροῦδης, εἰσοδανούσας τὸ σύζ-
γον Γιαννιωτζᾶ Παπάρη, ἐξήλθεν τὴν Μαρίναν καὶ τὴν
ἐνυμφεύθη πρὸ 9 μηνῶν, μετὰ 3 δὲ μῆνας μέλλει, διὰ δὲ
γοντος, νὰ γίνῃ μήτηρ· ὁ γαμβρός μας, ὃν θέλω νὰ γνωρίσ-
τε, εἶναι ἐνταλείόλατος καὶ ἐκ τῶν μεγαλυτέρων ἐμπόρων, ἀλλ'
ἔχει πολλὰ νεανία· τί νὰ γίνῃ ἐκ τῶν ὅλο ἡ τύχη μας, ἢ μᾶλλον
εὖ θερσολούσας οὕτω τὸ ἀνθρώπων.

(ἐπιστολὴ τοῦ ΔΗΜΗΤΡΙΟΥ ΜΠΑΡΜΠΑ ἀδελφοῦ τοῦ
φιλολόγου
ΙΩΑΝΝΟΥ καὶ χρήστου φαρμακοποιοῦ

16

John Delligeorges' Family: Our Story

From Perth, Australia

My other cousin, John Deligeorges, is the surviving son (his brother Emmanuel passed away in 2007) of my mother's younger sister, Elefteria, and her husband, Achilles. He and is wife, Eliane, live in Perth, Australia. They have two children: Joanne, who is married to Nic Damnjavonic now living in London, and Emmanuel who lives in Perth. Their story follows.

Elefteria with Emmanuel and
John Deligeorges in Cairo circa 1950.

I was born in Cairo, Egypt, on 3 May 1946, and in June 1951, a few years before Gamal Abdel Nasser came to power, my father Achilles, mother Elefteria and older brother Emmanuel and I left Egypt to immigrate to Australia. We embarked at Port Said on a British passenger liner named Oronsay with our destination being Perth in western Australia. The voyage lasted approximately two weeks, stopping once in Colombo in what was then Ceylon. We arrived in Perth after a stormy crossing of the Indian Ocean with all our worldly possessions in four pine boxes.

My Dad had chosen to follow his older brother Marcos and his family who had immigrated to Venezuela shortly before we left Egypt. In fact, we had already obtained Venezuelan visas; however, at the last minute, Dad chose Perth as our destination because a friend who travelled regularly to Perth where he had property investments extolled its beauty, climate and opportunities.

Dad was an automotive electrician by trade, although in Egypt he managed the transport arm of a cigarette company. Work in Perth was hard to find at first and for a while he was a chef in a café; later he found work as an auto mechanic. His friend generously gave us a block of land on the understanding that we only repay him if and when we could. Dad then literally built our first house, doing most of the work in the evenings and on weekends while working full time.

At first, life in Perth was harsh and strange, especially for my parents who were used to the cosmopolitan urban life of Cairo. In summer the heat, dust, flies and mosquitoes were intolerable.

My brother and I started school at ages six and five, respectively, knowing not one word of English but at that young age we picked it up quite quickly. We attended government schools—Como Primary and Applecross High School—as private schools were beyond my parents' means at the time.

Our lives as young children were uncomplicated. For amusement we would go hunting with slingshots and air-powered guns. We thought nothing of killing wildlife that today is protected and killing native fauna, including snakes and reptiles, which now incurs penalties running into thousands of dollars. In those days, people were all very trusting; no one locked their homes or cars. We had no drug problems or violent crimes and generally we lived in a safe, unpolluted semi-rural environment.

About the time we started high school, because my parents had no formal debt on their home, Dad was able to borrow against the house to buy a business running a Caltex Gas Station. It involved working from seven in the morning until seven in the evening and on weekends. So even us boys worked serving gas before and after school and on the weekends but my recollection is that we were a happy, close-knit family. We eventually became financially secure, quickly paying off the business loan and over a period of a few years, we acquired four additional homes.

In the mid-1960s, Dad had a serious heart attack and had to stop working. For a few more years, Mum and us boys were able to continue to run the business with the aid of one or two employees. Since Dad couldn't work, we convinced him to visit his gravely ill brother in Venezuela. As it was virtually halfway around the world, it was cheaper to buy an around-the-world ticket, which enabled him to also visit relatives in other countries. Sadly, while in Greece, he found out that his younger brother Vassili had died of a heart attack only days before his arrival.

After we relinquished the gas business, our parents leased a small apartment in Athens and lived for some years spending half the year there and half in Perth. Around 1970, Mum contracted breast cancer that eventually progressed to lung cancer and ultimately her death in 1975. It was a sad time, especially as I now realise how much she missed her siblings being isolated there without her family. After Mum died, Dad continued to live in Athens for half of each year. While holidaying in Leros, his father's birthplace, he suffered a massive heart attack and died. My brother and I flew to Leros for his funeral and burial. We later discovered that Greece exhumes remains after a number of years so my brother arranged for Dad's remains to be brought to Perth and be reburied in a perpetual grave alongside our mother.

My brother Emmanuel started studying accountancy part time in 1963 while working for a biscuit manufacturer and later worked for an American company that printed the Pink Pages phone directory (as the Yellow Pages were called then). When Emmanuel's employer lost the Pink Pages contract, they offered him a job in Singapore (as he was now a qualified accountant) with another arm of the parent company, Atwood Oceanics. It was there that he met and married his wife Sue. They eventually returned to Perth with both still working for Atwoods, which had opened a Perth operation.

My brother remained with Atwoods for the rest of his career. Sadly, he passed away 21 December 2007 after a long battle with cancer. His two children, Achilles and Eleftheria, are now in their twenties. Achilles studied teaching but is currently working casually as a tutor in Perth. Eleftheria completed a degree in mechanical engineering in Melbourne and is now working in Perth. His widow, Sue, spends a lot of her time managing a substantial property portfolio accumulated by my brother.

I was able to undertake a bachelor of arts degree in architecture at the University of Western Australia (UWA) between 1964 and 1968, having won a state government scholarship. During this period, I had the worry of having been drafted into the army because of the Vietnam conflict but call-up was deferred until the completion of my studies. In my final year, however, I failed the army medical exam and was not conscripted. In 1967, while still at university, I made a long road trip to Broome, beach resort in the north of our large state with several other students in a VW kombi-van. We went on to Darwin, down to Alice Springs then to Adelaide across to Kalgoorlie and back to Perth. It was probably one of the few times I had ventured outside Perth and it was an insight into the beauty and vastness of this country where you travel hundreds of miles without seeing a living thing. My parents, in fact never ventured outside the Perth metro area.

I worked as an architect for a government agency from 1969 to 197, after which I left for Europe on a two-year working holiday, employe mainly in London but also spending time travelling around Greece and most of Europe. In Greece, I was able to reunite with some of my mother's family who I had not seen since we left Egypt. This included Mum's older brother Uncle George, his wife Patra and son John who resided in Athens, Mum's younger sister Aunt Harriette and her husband Louis who had leased an apartment in Athens for an extensive vacation, and my Mum's younger brother Uncle Stavros who had come to Athens for a short stay. I have very fond memories of my time with family that previously I really only knew through the correspondence and photos Mum received from them over the years.

In 1974 while in London, I met my future wife Eliane Poirot who was taking a break from her language studies at the University of Nancy. We spent some time travelling together through Europe and in Greece where my parents still had an apartment. Eliane's family lived in the very picturesque Vosges Mountains in the east of France. We tried to get married in France but were thwarted by bureaucratic hurdles so we returned to Perth together and I married Eliane here in 1975. We were blessed with two children: Joanne, born 6 October 1977 and Emmanuel, born 28 April 1982.

When we returned to Perth, I again worked as a government architect and was involved in the design of municipal buildings, including the Art Gallery of Western Australia. I also designed the Atwood offices where my brother worked for the majority of his working life.

Over the years we made many trips back to Europe, mainly to visit Eliane's parents. They lived relatively close to Strassbourg where Uncle George told me he did his university studies and had developed a great liking for a local Alsatian white wine called Gewurztraminer. Eliane had a friend whose family owned a vineyard that grew this particular wine and on one trip to Greece we took a case of their wine to Uncle George.

The family story continues through the recollections of my children.

Joanne Deligeorges

I was christened Joanne Liberty Marie Deligeorges. The middle names reflect my paternal grandmother Elefteria (Greek for "liberty") and my maternal grandmother Marie. I had a wonderful childhood as the eldest child, as I had my parents all to myself until my little brother came along when I was five years of age.

My brother and I grew up living in one of the townhouses that my dad and uncle built in the 1980s after demolishing the original family home built by my grandfather in the 1950s. It was just back from the beautiful Swan River estuary, a vast expanse of water which, in those days, was unpolluted and where we would swim, fish and trawl for prawns and crabs. I have fond memories of fishing on the local jetty, riding bikes and climbing trees with local neighbourhood kids. I recall that Dad built a miniature pine cottage I named Rose Cottage and a billycart I called Red Lightening, which got some serious mileage around nearby hilly streets.

We used to go to France periodically over the school summer holidays to visit our maternal grandparents who lived only 70 kilometers from the German border. On one trip, I remember going with Dad, just the two of us, on a road trip to pick up a slick black Audi he had rented from just on the other side of the border (it was much cheaper to rent cars in Germany than in France). It also gave Dad an excuse to go mad on the Autobahns, which had no speed limits. I am certain my bother inherited his love of fast cars from Dad.

I remember my Papou who passed away in 1985 when I was only eight years old. Sadly, my paternal grandmother died before I was born. I still have a jewellery box and a little bag Papou gave to me. He was an avid traveller and I still have a beautiful cushion cover that he bought in Venezuela. From a young age I treasured this and other things of his which I have kept even after all the culling of possessions we have had to make with our many relocations over the years.

I loved sports and Dad noticed I was quite adept at tennis from a young age, so he encouraged me to start playing competitively from the age of six. I played almost every Saturday during the summer months with a fair degree of success as a junior player. I recall the prize for winning one competition was tickets to a Davis Cup tie between Australia and France. At the event, I got to meet and hit up with Yannick Noah, one of my favourite tennis players of the time. I also played netball with a significantly less success. Our team coach was our Dad; this was a gender-busting role as coaches at that time were without exception Mums. Dad always encouraged us in sport but also instilled the importance of education, although I have minimal recollections of being harassed to study.

I did surprisingly well at high school and for this I have a huge debt of gratitude to Mum and Dad for the genetic blessing. Dad was far too humble to admit that he had a real talent for art. Mum raised us with enough exposure to French for me to excel in French studies. With excellent tertiary entrance exam results, I qualified to undertake a combined bachelor of law/arts at UWA from 1995 to 1999. This is the same university from which my Dad, brother and husband have graduated. Without prejudice, UWA is the oldest and most beautiful campus in Perth. It is set in lush gardens and situated on the shores of the Swan River.

Towards the end of my first year at university, I met my future husband Nicolas Jacques Damnjanovic. It was love at first sight and we married very young the following year in 1996. Nic, being a year older, had already completed one a year of medicine but decided to change to philosophy, which he pursued until finally completing a PhD at the Australian National University. After this, he worked as a philosophy academic for several years both in Australia and Colorado. Nic's family tree is quite interesting. Mum's maiden name was Lyn Winter and she is a direct descendant of the Winter involved in the failed gunpowder plot, in which a group of provincial English Catholics led by Robert Catesby attempted to assassinate King James I of England in 1605. The Damnjanovic name comes from Nic's dad's stepfather Boris Damn-

Joanne and Nic in Canberra, Australia circa 2003

janovic. Boris was a Croatian refugee who married Nic's already pregnant French grandmother after they met in an Italian refugee camp at the
end of World War II. Nic's grandmother never revealed who was Nic's
biological grandfather. We suspect he was either French or German giv-
en the times but we like to think he was French, thus making Nic half-
French, the same as me.

Nic and I contemplated starting a family; however, for a combination of health issues and career choices, this didn't eventuate or wasn't
meant to be but we are now really very content with our lives. I secured
a position as a prosecutor with the Western Australia Directorate of Public Prosecutions and I worked there for several years (2000 to 2003)
until we moved to Canberra for Nic to undertake a PhD at the Australian
National University (ANU) and where I secured similar prosecutor position to the one I held in Perth.

We lived in Canberra while Nic studied and I worked (from 2003 to 2005). While there we took up Tai Chi. As fate would have it, the descendants of a prestigious and famous Tai Chi lineage had started an academy in Canberra. Canberra had its shortcomings, including harsher weather and a somewhat more sterile environment than Perth, but one great advantage was its proximity to Sydney where Nic's family on his father's side lived.

Nic and I then moved to Melbourne where we lived from 2005 to 2007 before returning to Perth, where I resumed working as a lawyer and Nic won a post teaching philosophy at UWA, eventually advancing to acting head of department. At some point, we decided that Nic would make a fantastic lawyer and so he undertook a bachelor of laws degree while holding his academic position in the arts faculty. On completion, he joined the State Solicitor's Office (the civil equivalent of the DA's office). We bought a house in Perth in 2012 and we both continued practicing law. Once we had paid off our house loan and had decided not to have children, we decided it would shake things up in our lives to move to the UK. So in 2015, when Nic was offered a place in a prestigious law course at Oxford, we relocated once again. We lived in Oxford, a magical place, for about a year before moving to London in 2016 when Nic finished his studies. Oxford was an unforgettable experience and we were so glad we made the move.

We initially planned to return to Perth but Nic was very fortunate to be invited to join Fountain Court Chambers initially under tutelage and later as a full barrister. These prestigious chambers are located in the legal district in London called Temple where the buildings and traditions go back to the days of the Knights Templar. Working in this profession, in this environment and in one of the most exciting cities on the planet was an opportunity Nic couldn't pass up so we decided to settle in London for the foreseeable future. As a result, we sold our home in Perth and are currently looking to invest in a home in London.

I recently started working at Yamamoto Keiko Rochaix Gallery, a contemporary gallery in Whitechapel mainly to gain some experience and insight of the art world, as well as networking with people in this industry. I also have a few design projects I aim to pursue, including some lighting and furniture design concepts. At this writing, we have just returned from a tour of Rome and Palermo which, apart from being a great holiday, was inspirational for an art lover like me.

Emmanuel Deligeorges

Unlike Joanne, I have spent most of my life in Perth. I was born 28 April 1982. I attended Como and St. Columba's primary schools then completed my secondary education at Aquinas College in 1999. I went on to complete a combined science/civil engineering degree at UWA in 2004.

From 2005 to 2008, I worked as a salaried geotechnical engineer with Knight Pisold and Associates. While in this job I spent a lot of time in Laos, where I realised I was not really interested in working for long periods in the remote regions of foreign countries.

I then had the good fortune to be invited to join a consortium of geotechnical engineers where I basically have operated my own business since 2008. One of the benefits of being self-employed is choosing where and when I work. I made a policy to only accept site work within Australia.

I am now 36 and although still unmarried I have had several long-term relationships but I guess I am not quite ready to make the plunge. My great passion is fast cars and with generous support from my parents when I was younger I have been fortunate to own a string of fast exotic cars. I currently own a high-powered Audi Q5 SUV, a classic BMW M3 and my latest acquisition is a fantastic Audi R8. I immensely enjoy driving each of them.

17

Nicholas' Poetry

AN UNSPOKEN EMOTION

I admire your face,
so serene with sentiment
It is as beautiful as nature itself.

And when a shadow of grief is cast upon it,
I would like to give you my hand
And raise you up out of the pit of despair,
And into the garden of life,
Were roses grow thornless,
And flowers never wither.

But alas, my sentimental friend,
My pen is but mortal,
And can only give you the strength
of words on paper,
Which went or alas fails,
Are always by your side.

THE BEAUTY OF A SUNSET

The beauty of the sunset
Lies not in its colors,
But on how beautiful it
Illuminates the day's events.
For if we do not remember how beautiful life is today
Why look forward to tomorrow?

SPRING

I was born in a white washed cottage
Set on top of a bluff
Which gazed serenely at a deep blue Bay,
With hills arising on the other side
Like the early morning sun

I grew up among on those thyme-scented Hills
Which carry the smell of civilization past
And walking along those ivory colored beaches
I would relive the glory of my ancestors.

At night I used to sleep on my ivory beach
With my blue-eyed mistress by my side,
And while her cool Long fingers lapped slowly at my face
She would reveal to me the poetry of nature.

In the morning my mistress would beckon me
to the refreshing presence of her being
And with her emissaries the dolphins
She would show me her never ending secrets.

Come went to that I went into the city,
To work like every man should do,
but my heart is a swinging dolphin
Which longs for the birth of nature spring

NOW

How often do you forget now?
How often do you forget to
kiss the ones we love,
whisper love to the ones we love,
caress the ones we love,
cry for the ones we love,
or live for the ones we love.

How often do we forget to
smell a rose,
catch a star,
smell fresh air,
sing with a Bird,
laugh with a friend,
or smile with small children.

how often do we forget that
Life is now
it is not tomorrow,
or the next day,
Or next year,
it is not business meetings,
exams,
financial statements,
doctors appointment,
and it is definitely not
the state of economy!

How often do you forget that
Now that does not take,
It lasts a moment,

And does not take time away
from of those other things.

In the mist of all clocked time,
now is untimed;
It does not last, a second
It simply is a moment.
How often do we forget that
moments of Now is the substance of life,
everything else,
pain, sufferings,
boredom, excitement,
Work, and play,
only serve to tie
one moment to another.
Moments are the measure
of life,
moments are shared,
they're given,
They are lived;
They are life.

So next time Remember
When a stranger asks you the Time,
smile, take their hand,
and say,
"Our time is Now;
The moment is Now."

PART SIX

Ancestry Tree

Due to the large size of the full family tree, only a portion of it is shown here.

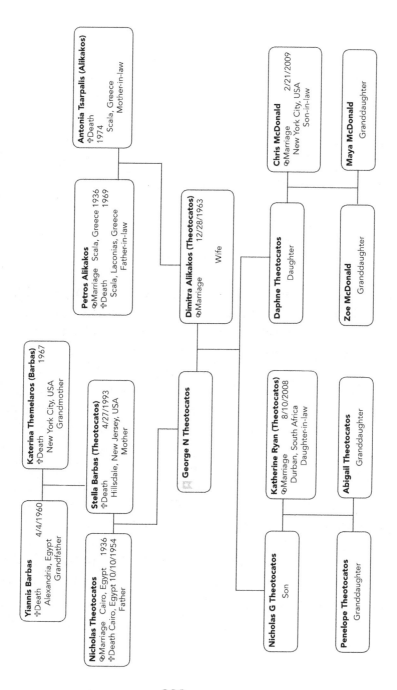

ACKNOWLEDGMENTS

I am indebted to several people who helped bring this book to life. Their support made my task easier and fun.

I am thankful to my friends, Sharon Eakes and Hugh Leonard, for their encouragement and support in the early writing stages. Their guidance on the technical aspects of writing and publishing has been invaluable.

Special thanks to my brother, Takis, for his encouragement, enthusiasm and help in translating our father's short stories and also sharing his own extraordinary story.

I am grateful to my family: my wife, Dimitra, and my daughter, Daphne, who stood by me and gave me the courage and support to start and complete my story; and to my son, Nicholas, for allowing me to include his poems, thereby adding a literary content to the narrative.

I am indebted to my cousins, John Barbas and John Deligeorges, and his daughter, Joanne, who shared their life stories and, by doing so, added an international collaborative dimension to the family odyssey.

My appreciation goes to my editor, Gina Mazza, who understood my mission and guided me through the process of enlivening the manuscript. Her editorial comments, gently yet firmly, made the process easier and resulted in what you have in your hands now.

And finally, I am grateful for my four beautiful granddaughters—Penelope, Zoe, Maya and Abigail— for being the inspiration to write these pages and expanding my capacity to love.

ABOUT THE AUTHOR

 George Theotocatos is a former Exxon Company executive with nearly 30 years of service with the organization in New York and New Jersey corporate offices and abroad. Almost half of his career was spent in the Middle East, holding executive positions in Planning, Projects Management and Commercial Operations in Libya, Saudi Arabia and Abu Dhabi. He has travelled extensively in the Middle East, Asia and South America.

After retirement from Exxon, he was invited by the East West Center at the University of Hawaii in Honolulu as a visiting scholar to participate in a leadership program coaching future leaders to create a better world. He now lives with his wife in East Hampton, New York.

George can be reached at gtheoto@yahoo.com.

Made in the USA
Middletown, DE
26 February 2019